100
ways to
enhance
self-
concept
in the
class-
room

Jack Canfield
Self-Esteem Seminars

Harold C. Wells
National University

PRENTICE-HALL, INC., ENGLEWOOD CLIFFS, NEW JERSEY

100 ways to enhance self-concept in the class-room

a handbook for teachers and parents

Library of Congress Cataloging in Publication Data

Canfield, Jack, (date)
    100 ways to enhance self-concept in the classroom.

    (Prentice-Hall curriculum and teaching series)
    Bibliography: p.
    1. Motivation in education. 2. Self-actualization
(Psychology) 3. Self-respect. I. Wells, Harold C.,
(date) joint author. II. Title.
LB1065.C26   370.15'4   75-20314
ISBN 0-13-636951-0
ISBN 0-13-636944-8 pbk.

PRENTICE-HALL CURRICULUM AND TEACHING SERIES
Ronald T. Hyman, *series editor*

100 Ways to Enhance Self-Concept in the Classroom: a handbook for teachers and parents
by Jack Canfield and Harold C. Wells

Printed in the United States of America

Current printing (last digit):

25 24 23 22 21 20

*We wish to acknowledge many publishers and individuals
for their permission to reprint materials in this book;
since there is insufficient space to accommodate them here,
we have done so beginning on page 245.*

Prentice-Hall International, Inc., London
Prentice-Hall of Australia, Pty. Ltd, Sydney
Prentice-Hall of Canada, Ltd., Toronto
Prentice-Hall of India Private Limited, New Delhi
Prentice-Hall of Japan, Inc., Tokyo
Prentice-Hall of Southeast Asia (Pte.) Ltd., Singapore

This book is dedicated to
teachers, parents and everyone else in the world
concerned with helping children develop
a true sense of themselves
as lovable and capable human beings.

contents

two
my strengths 89

three
who am I? 113

four

accepting my body   147

five

where am I going?   171

foreword

This book is an absolute delight! It is, indeed, a gold mine for teachers but it deserves a better metaphor than that cliche. It is more like cherry pie with so many damn cherries you can't get your fork through to the crust or pistachio ice cream so nutty no cone can handle it.

Jack Canfield and Harold Wells have compiled some of the sweetest, most gentle, most instantly useful and gripping exercises, strategies and techniques ever put between the covers of a book. Their long, their life-long, experiences with the humanistic education movement and their dedication to the notion that *positiveness* makes people grow illuminates every page of this book. The book glows and shines.

I warn you about one vital thing. Don't you dare read this book in summer, or on vacation or on Friday night of a long weekend. The results could be dangerous. Why? And well you might ask. Why? Because you won't be able to stand the ordeal of not having your students in front of you to try out everything, immediately, in this exciting, practical and deeply inspiring book. Be well warned.

The average teacher will find the concise clarity of the descriptions of each strategy almost magical. These writers don't just talk. It is apparent that they've DONE these exercises and they believe in them. (I would like to make an important cautionary note here. I, personally, urge every teacher using the strategies and techniques which Canfield and Wells have put before you here with such gem-like perfection to try the techniques, FIRST, on your own life and experiences. That is, do the strategy and see what it brings out about your own life, before you try these on other peoples' children. That seems like a decent enough ethical demand to make of you.)

This book is a lot more than just exercises, although there are, indeed, 100, count them, 100 beautiful examples of how to build a validating, searching positive and success-oriented community in any classroom.

The book includes an excellent bibliography which demonstrates how well grounded Canfield and Wells are in the humanistic education field. There is also a guide to all kinds of resources. The back of the book becomes almost a road-map for an individual teacher's growth. There are places to write to for curriculum guides and there is a very useful guide to growth centers and other places where teachers can learn, stretch and, hopefully, more fully come to reach their own very beautiful potential.

The profession needs, desperately, more practical, demonstratedly successful classroom materials like the ones so artfully brought together by Jack Canfield and Harold Wells. I am proud to be able to recommend this one so warmly.

It belongs in the Christmas stocking of every teacher in America. But, oops, remember my warning. They won't have their students in front of them to try out the strategies if they get this book at Christmas. A warning could be put on the cover of every copy. **"CAUTION: Do Not read unless teaching this day."** It would be just too frustrating to read the ideas and not have those live minds in front of you. Maybe a better idea would be if every Superintendent of Schools put one in every teachers' mailbox on the first day of school in September. If not then, then in January. The book is that great. Use it tenderly. And watch your self-concept grow. Joy.

Professor of Humanistic Education, University of Massachusetts
School of Education, Amherst, Massachusetts 01002

California has just completed a statewide school/community by school/community goals process. Not surprisingly, every school/community placed reading, writing and arithmetic among its primary goals for its children. Surprisingly, every school/community declared that self esteem/concept is also among its primary goals for its children.

This addition of self esteem as a fourth major goal of education is monumental. It signals a revolutionary cultural reversal from self-denial to self-actualization. But it is a revolution in the best American sense—for it signals as well the embodiment of, and foundation for realizing, the dream of our founding fathers, real self-determination. The first line of the first section of the California Constitution even reads: "All persons are by nature free and independent." And it is hopeful because learning is a function of self esteem, as are life and health and humanness itself.

So the emerging major task in education today is to define self esteem, and to discover the process by which it is nurtured. This book is timely and vital in that it speaks precisely to that task, by proposing methods for the nurturance of self esteem.

The book is especially fine because it breaks out of our old cultural traps of founding self esteem in having or doing. Those lead to the materialistic and performance mores that are at best substitutional, at worst downright unhealthy for the human. Rather it recognizes, as each of us must, that the ultimate in self esteem is found in the full possession of one's total being—the intellect and the emotions and (especially) the body—in other words, in the ultimate right of the human being—the right to be one's self.

Finally though, as fine as the book is, it can be only a tool. It's use depends upon you—and you can't give what you haven't got. How you utilize these methods will depend upon your own self esteem. Only if you are truly into your own being, possess and value yourself, feel comfortable with and good about yourself, believe in and live your right to be yourself—will you truly enhance self esteem in those young human beings whose self esteem, whose lives, are touched by you.

John Vasconcellos
Chairman of the Joint Legislative Committee on Educational Goals and Evaluation
Member of the California Legislature

preface

This is intended to be a *practical* book. We hope that it is practical in that it truly does contain over one-hundred techniques which are designed to enhance one's sense of identity and self-esteem and which have been classroom tested at all grade levels from kindergarten through college. We hope that it is also practical in that it contains some theory, but only enough to provide a solid foundation for each of the various activities and not enough to get bogged down in!

We believe that teachers, college professors, education students, principals, psychologists, church school teachers and parents (anyone who works with people in groups!) will find this book a valuable resource of ideas that will help them in the creation of learning environments that are positive, caring, supportive, and growth promoting.

We are convinced that one of the major challenges to teachers and other group leaders is the creation of a self-enhancing learning environment. Some special people seem to do this quite naturally out of their own authentic being and their commitment to others. Most of us, however, benefit from specific, usable suggestions that help us toward that end. It is in that spirit that these activities were designed and compiled.

We are deeply indebted to a great many friends and colleagues for the ideas and activities found in this book, however, many of these people are actually unknown to us—as the activities were told to us by someone who had experienced them in a group, or we heard about them "second hand" from someone who had read about them, and so on. We certainly have no intention of crediting ourselves with the development of many of these exercises—although some are ours—so when we're quite sure of the source we acknowledge that person. It is the nature of the whole humanistic movement in the helping professions that we "borrow" from one another freely, and that seems perfectly sensible to us. However, we regret being generally unable to tie specific activities to specific authors. In any event, we are grateful indeed to both our known and unknown associates in the grand endeavor of building a better world!

As you might imagine, we have become addicted activity collectors. If you discover, invent, or create new variations on activities we would greatly appreciate your sharing them with us. Any contributions we use in future publications will be faithfully acknowledged. , Please send them to us at Self-Esteem Seminars, 17156 Palisades Circle, Pacific Palisades, CA 90272.

ACKNOWLEDGMENTS

Acknowledging all of the people responsible for this book is a difficult job. There have been so many who have guided us, inspired us, offered us suggestions, shared their wisdom with us, sent us exercises, tried things out in their classrooms and critiqued the manuscript of this book. There are certainly still others who have influenced us in ways too subtle to note, and yet, if we had not known them, this book would certainly not be the same.

We would particularly like to acknowledge and thank W. Clement Stone, Billy B. Sharp, Lacy Hall, and Jim Nugent, whose offices we shared when we conceived this book. Without their pioneering work in self-concept and their trust in us, we most probably never would have met, let alone written this book. Lacy Hall especially provided continued encouragement and support.

We would like to pay tribute to Herbert Otto, Arthur Combs, Earl Kelley, Fritz Perls, Abraham Maslow, and Roberto Assagioli, all of whom provided valuable theoretical frameworks from which our own work has developed.

We are especially grateful to our own teachers who have given selflessly of their time to us, encouraged us, prodded us to deeper and broader understandings of our subject, and most importantly, loved us. They include Jack Gibb, Gerald Weinstein, Sidney Simon, Al Alschuler, George Brown, Bob Resnick, William C. Miller, Gurushabd Singh Josephs, Martha Crampton, and our children, Oran David Canfield and Susan, Ann, and Todd Wells, who have taught us in their own ways.

We can probably never repay our wives, Judy Ohlbaum-Canfield and Dolores Wells, for their sharing their husbands with a book for two years. Their tolerance for our late night writing sessions was remarkable and greatly appreciated.

Many people provided exercises for this book. Where known, they are acknowledged at the end of the activity. We feel especially indebted to Sidney Simon, John Stevens, Gerald Weinstein, James Foley, Doris Shallcross, Martha Crampton, Billy B. Sharp, Lacy Hall, Herbert Otto, Marlowe Berg, Patricia Wolleat, Audrey Peterson, and Elizabeth Achterman, all of whom allowed us to borrow freely from their work. Victor Miller, Jim Fadiman and Judy Ohlbaum-Canfield provided extensive and useful critiques of our manuscript. We are indebted to them for their corrections and additions.

It seems that books these days are no longer simply written; they are produced by a great number of people. We want to especially acknowledge Adrienne Neufeld and Lorraine Mullaney at Prentice-Hall who continually helped us mold our conglomeration of typewritten pages, notes, memos, corrections, and art work into the wonderfully arranged and complete book that this is.

We also wish to thank Alan Lipp and Nancy Bair who spent countless hours typing the final manuscript, and Elaine Rapp, Janet Goto, Paula Klimek, and Ginny Duff for supplying us with needed, last-minute photographs during the final phases of production.

Finally, we want to thank the thousands of teachers who have been in our workshops and our classes, and who have tried out these exercises in their classrooms and reported their experiences to us. Their feedback has been invaluable.

Jack Canfield, *Amherst, Massachusetts*
Harold C. Wells, *San Diego, California*

One of the great tragedies of people's lives is that, in denying and repressing their inner emotional experience, they submerge in the underground of their subconscious not only their fear and their pain but their creative potential for the enjoyment of life. Psychologists like to boast of their skill at detecting men's hidden vices—I have always found it much more interesting and challenging to unearth their hidden virtues.

Nathaniel Branden
The Psychology of Self-Esteem

That's what's needed don't you see, that . . . nothing else matters half so much . . . to reassure one another, to answer each other. Perhaps only you can listen to me and not laugh. Everyone has inside himself . . . what shall I call it—a piece of good news. Everyone is a very great and important character. Yes, that's what we have to tell them. Every man must be persuaded, even if he's in rags, that he is immensely, immensely important. Everyone must respect him and make him respect himself, too. They must listen to him attentively—don't stand on top of him, don't stand in his light, but look at him with gentleness, deference, give him great, great hopes, he needs them, especially if he's young—spoil him. Yes, make him grow proud.

Ugo Betti
Burnt Flower Bed (an Italian play)

I had a great feeling of relief when I began to understand that a youngster needs more than just subject matter. Oh, I know mathematics well, and I teach it well. I used to think that that was all I needed to do. Now I teach children, not math. I accept the fact that I can only succeed partially with some of them. I have found further that my own personhood has educatable value. When I don't have to know all the answers, I seem to have more answers than before when I tried to be the expert. The youngster who really made me understand this was Eddie. I asked him one day why he thought he was doing so much better than last year. He gave meaning to my whole new orientation. "It's because I like myself now when I'm with you," he said.

A teacher quoted by Everett Shostrom in
Man, the Manipulator

introduction: self-concept in teaching and learning

I am happy. I am sick. I am good. I am beautiful.
I'm a loser. I'm a winner. I am dumb. I am fine.
I'm okay. I am bad. I am clumsy. I am a gossip.
I'm neurotic. I am a bore. I'm a mess. I'm cool.
I am successful. I'm a failure. I'm lovable. I'm sexy.
I am sad. I'm smart. I am a good teacher.
I am a good person. I'm a slow learner. I'm not okay.

Which of these sentences describe you? Go back and draw a circle around each sentence that expresses how you feel most of the time. Go ahead. Do it now.

How many of your circled sentences please you? There are twenty-six sentences: thirteen that are essentially "positive" and thirteen "negative." When you look at your responses in this light, what kind of picture do you get of yourself? That picture is a little glimpse of a tiny part of your *self-concept*!

Your self-concept is composed of all the beliefs and attitudes you have about yourself. They actually determine *who you are*! They also determine *what* you think you are, what you *do,* and what you can *become*!

It's amazing to think that these internal beliefs and attitudes you hold about yourself are that powerful; but they are. In fact, in a very functional sense, they are your *Self*.

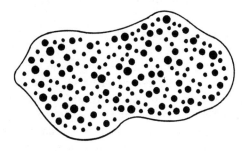

*Parts of this introduction originally appeared in "Self-Concept: A Critical Dimension in Teaching and Learning," by Jack Canfield and Harold C. Wells in *Humanistic Education Handbook,* ed. Donald M. Read and Sidney B. Simon (Englewood Cliffs, N.J.: Prentice-Hall, Inc., 1975).

Imagine the "glob" on page 1 as a representation of your Self. You are an entity that hangs together in an organized, consistent, reasonably firm and permanent state, yet you also have the quality of fluidity—something like a strong jellyfish! The dots in the glob represent the thousands of beliefs you hold about yourself. They fit together in a meaningful pattern or "system," each complementing the others so that they form an integrated whole.

Notice that some of the dots are more "internal" than others. The more central a belief is to your Self, the more value—either negative or positive—you attach to it. For example, most teachers feel that to be smart is more important than to be a good swimmer. (Not everyone feels that way.) Most teachers' beliefs and attitudes about their own intelligence, then, are more central in their Self systems than their beliefs and attitudes about their swimming ability.

HOW IS THE SELF FORMED?

It is evident that the Self is learned. It is not inherited. From our earliest moments of life we begin to accumulate data about ourselves and our world. New impressions flood in upon us. We soon learn what eases pain and what makes us comfortable, what satisfies our hunger, what it takes to get attention, and so on. As our experiences multiply, our developing Self becomes a perceptual screen through which subsequent impressions must pass. For example, if an infant has been fed at the breast for weeks, he will not be satisfied with a spoon. His perceptual screen will reject the spoon as the wrong shape, and too hard and cold, and he will scream for the object he *knows* is right!

In the same manner we gradually formulate impressions and attitudes about ourselves. A crawling baby reaches out to grasp a figurine on a low coffee table. The mother says, "No, no, no! Mustn't touch. Bad boy!" Repeated exposure to such responses teach the child—"I do things wrong. Things are more important than I am. I'm bad!" This, of course, is not at all what the parent wanted to teach, but nevertheless is precisely the message that many infants receive in such situations.

This example illustrates how vitally important early childhood experiences are in forming the kind of persons we become. We are especially vulnerable to the responses we get from our parents (particularly mother) because of the amount of time spent with them and our total dependence on them.

THE SELF IS CONSISTENT

Let's return to our illustration of the "glob." Any new experience you have is interpreted in light of all the beliefs and attitudes you've accumulated within your Self. If a new experience is consistent with what you believe, it is enveloped and your Self becomes a little larger. On the other hand, if the new experience is not consistent with your Self, it is ignored or rejected. Your "glob" simply withdraws a little where the new experience hits and moves right on past it, filling itself in as though nothing has occurred. This is a wonderful protective quality, actually. It keeps us together! There are some problems with it, however. It makes change in self-concept extremely difficult because to *significantly change anything* requires modification of the whole system in order to retain a consistency of Self. Here is an illustration of this concept:

> Jack is a good kid. He's a typical boy, so he sometimes gets into little scrapes, but never anything too bad. However, on this occasion Jack is playing with some other boys and they decide to steal some cigarettes and hide somewhere and smoke them. Jack is scared, but excited, too. Jack's little brother hears about what has happened and tells their father, who raises the roof with poor Jack. What does Jack say? What does he *really* believe about this incident? "I didn't want to steal but—well, the gang kind of—you know. Besides *I* didn't steal the cigarettes. Charley did! I only smoked one and I hated it. It was a good lesson. I'll never smoke those awful things again."

Sounds like a lot of kids you know, doesn't it? Now why did Jack respond like this? It's simple, really. Jack, *just as every other human being alive, must protect his self-esteem—his feelings about himself.* He did that in this instance by rationalizing about being kind of "forced" into the situation and by figuring what a great lesson it was. He may, in time, actually come to believe he did it as an experiment; a lesson to himself on how bad cigarettes taste so he'll never again be tempted by the habit. See how smart that makes him, and how good he can feel about himself? So, two things have happened. First, Jack's image of himself as a "good kid" is retained. He has taken an objectively "bad" incident and filtered it through his Self system in such a way as to maintain this consistency of his concept of himself. Second—and this is closely related—he has maintained or increased his self-esteem. *This is the prime motivation for all "normal" behavior.* It is perhaps our most important ability as human beings. We must, in spite of everything, be able to accept our own behavior. The strangest, most bizarre, and often most hideous behavior can be accounted for by this motivation to maintain and enhance one's Self *in one's own eyes.*

It is difficult for others to see how some behavior can possibly be Self-maintaining—but it is. We would have to be inside the skin of the other person to fully comprehend his actions, which of course is not possible, but we can keep this idea in mind and try to probe for data that will help us understand his rationale, no matter how distorted it may seem in *our* eyes.

LEARNING AND SELF-CONCEPT

By the time a child reaches school age his self-concept is quite well formed and his reactions to learning, to school failure and success, and to the physical, social, and emotional climate of the classroom will be determined by the beliefs and attitudes he has about himself. There is considerable evidence to support this view. Perhaps the most dramatic is that of Wattenberg and Clifford,[1] who studied kindergarten youngsters in an attempt to see if self-concept was predic-

---

[1] W. W. Wattenberg and C. Clifford, *Relationship of Self Concept to Beginning Achievement in Reading,* U.S. Office of Education, Cooperative Research Project No. 377 (Detroit: Wayne State University, 1962).

tive of reading success two and a half years later. It was. In fact, it was a better predictor than IQ! Children with low (poor) self-concepts did not learn to read or did not read as well as children with high (good) self-concepts.

Other studies affirm the position that self-concept is related to achievement in school; they also indicate that the relationship is particularly strong in boys, that it begins to make itself evident as early as the first grade, and that learning difficulties experienced in early school years persist.

WHAT YOU CAN DO
ABOUT STUDENTS' SELF-CONCEPTS

Theory is helpful, but the heart of the matter is what we can **do** about students' self-concepts. We can extract several principles from what has been said above:

1. **It is possible to change self-concepts, and it is possible for teachers to effect the changes—either way, both positive and negative.**

   Many of us teach because we had a teacher or two who really had a significant impact on us. The impact was related to our self-concept. The teacher somehow communicated a sense of caring and a sense of our own personal worth. On the other hand, many of us have also experienced a teacher who humiliated us or our classmates through sarcasm and ridicule. These teachers make learning a negative experience. Teachers can and do effect pupils' self-concepts every day. You have a choice over what kind of effect you will have.

2. **It isn't easy. Change takes place slowly, over a long period of time.**

   This is not written to discourage you, obviously, but simply to caution you not to expect sudden and dramatic changes in the way a child feels about himself. Self-concept builds the same way muscles do, slowly and often, at first, imperceptibly.

3. **Efforts that aim at more central beliefs have greater impact on the student even though they are harder to change.**

   Our society puts very heavy emphasis on academic ability. If you can help the child see himself as capable of learning you are dealing with a central belief. If you help a mischievous boy see himself as kind and helpful, or a doubting girl see herself as intelligent and attractive, you've made a significant difference in the life of the child.

4. **Peripheral experiences are helpful.**

   Many successes are required to help a person feel better about himself in a basic sense. The development of talents is important, for example. Almost anything you do, from calling a student by his name to complimenting him on his new shoes helps to create a sense of self-worth.

5. **Relating successes or strengths to one another is important.**

   You can strengthen the impact of any enhancing experience by relating it to others the student has had. For example, when a child produces a good piece of art work, you can say, "I really like your picture, Harold. You learned to use charcoal very quickly, I noticed!" This relates his artistic talent to what may be a more central belief about himself—his ability to learn.

There are some additional things you can do about pupils' self-concepts. Perhaps most important is creating an environment of mutual support and caring. Soar[2] has shown that growth is optimized in a supportive environment that contains a little dissonance. For the most part we don't have to create dissonance deliberately—there is usually more than enough to go around! The crucial thing, however, is the safety and encouragement students sense in the classroom. They must trust other group members and the teacher to the extent that they can truly express their feelings openly without ridicule or derision. Further, they must recognize that they are valued and will receive affection and support. This can't be stated strongly enough. Without the critical environmental dimensions of trust, caring, and openness the teacher's efforts to enhance pupils' sense of self-esteem will be seriously limited.

CREATING AN OPEN, CARING ENVIRONMENT

The subject of the creation of an open and caring environment could well be a book in itself! We can only outline some of the more important concepts here.

Let's start with the basic teacher-pupil relationship. Abraham Maslow described the self-actualizing teacher with these words:

> Our teacher-subjects behaved in a very unneurotic way simply by interpreting the whole situation differently, i.e., as a pleasant collaboration rather than as a clash of wills, of authority, of dignity, etc. The replacement of artificial dignity—which is easily and inevitably threatened—with the natural simplicity which is *not* easily threatened; the giving up of the attempt to be omniscient and omnipotent; the absence of student-threatening authoritarianism, the refusal to regard the students as competing with each other or with the teacher; the refusal to assume the "professor" stereotype and the insistence on remaining as realistically human as, say a plumber or a carpenter; all of these created a classroom atmosphere in which suspicion, wariness, defensiveness, hostility, and anxiety disappeared.[3]

This sets the direction for us. We must strive for a natural, human, democratic relationship. This means involving students from the beginning in creating the environment. They must help in decision-making about the physical setting (the arranging of the room, care for equipment, bulletin boards, etc.). Students also must be involved in planning the academic environment. This includes decisions about content, sequence of activities, and even methods of study. All this must take place within the limits defined by school district policies, of course, but these too must be openly acknowledged and confronted.

---

[2] S. Robert Soar, "Humanizing Secondary Schools," unpublished paper (mimeograph) distributed by the Institute for Development of Human Resources, University of Florida, College of Education, Gainesville, Florida, 1968.

[3] Abraham H. Maslow, "Self-Actualizing People: A Study of Psychological Health," in Clark E. Moustakas, *The Self: Explorations in Personal Growth* (New York: Harper and Row, 1956), pp. 190-91.

Students have a vested interest in the emotional environment of the classroom as well. Teachers and students should sit down together and freely discuss cooperation and competition, trust and fear, openness and deceit, and so on. These and many other topics discussed in classroom meetings help create the kind of climate that fosters total pupil growth.

Additional factors that appear to contribute to a "positive" classroom milieu are enumerated by us in our self-concept-self-identity curriculum,[4] in which elements of a supportive classroom climate are cited as including such important teacher behaviors as:

1. Accepting pupil contributions without judgment
2. Maintaining a "you can do it" attitude
3. Listening, listening, listening
4. Being, in all ways, a friend

It is interesting to compare this brief treatment of this subject with Hamachek's[5] summary of the research on qualities of effective teachers:

We can sketch at least five interrelated generalizations from what research is telling us about how effective teachers differ from less effective teachers when it comes to perceptions of others. In relation to this, effective teachers can be characterized in the following ways:

1. They seem to have a generally more positive view of others—students, colleagues, and administrators.
2. They are not prone to view others as critical, attacking people with ulterior motives, but rather see them as potentially friendly and worthy in their own right.
3. They have a more favorable view of democratic classroom procedures.
4. They have the ability and capacity to see things as they seem to others, i.e., the ability to see things from the other person's point of view.
5. They do not see students as persons "you do things to" but rather as individuals capable of doing for themselves once they feel trusted, respected, and valued.

If you as a teacher behave in a way consistent with the principles and characteristics enumerated in this introduction, your teaching will build children rather than destroy them! Is there anything more important?

THE RELATIONSHIP OF SELF-CONCEPT TO LEARNING

One of the questions often asked by teachers regards the relationship of self-concept to the learning of subject matter. The research literature is filled

---

[4] Harold C. Wells and Jack Canfield, *About Me,* Teacher's Guide (425 North Michigan Avenue, Chicago, Ill.: Encyclopedia Britannica Educational Corp., 1971), p. 76.
[5] Donald E. Hamachek, *Encounter with the Self* (New York: Holt, Rinehart and Winston, 1971), p. 202.

with reports indicating that cognitive learning increases when self-concept increases. The data suggesting this conclusion is quite extensive and overwhelming.[6]

We have developed a theory to explain this phenomenon which we call the "poker chip theory of learning." We see all learning as the result of a risk-taking situation somewhat akin to a poker game (or any other gambling situation, for that matter). In any potential learning situation, the student is asked to take a risk: to write a paper that will be evaluated, to make a recitation which may be laughed at, to do board work that may be wrong, to create an object of art that might be judged, etc. In each situation he is risking error, judgment, disapproval, censure, rejection, and, in extreme cases, even punishment. At a deeper level the student is risking his or her self-concept.

Imagine that each student's self-concept is a stack of poker chips. Some students start the learning game, as it were, with a lot of poker chips; others with very few. The students with the higher number of chips have a great advantage. To continue the poker analogy, the student with one hundred chips can sustain twenty losses of five chips each. The student with only fifteen chips can only sustain three losses of five chips each. The latter student will be much more cautious and reticent about stepping into the arena. This kind of student manifests a variety of behaviors indicating his reluctance to risk learning. They range from "This is stupid, I don't want to do it" (translation: "I am stupid; I'm afraid I can't do it") and withdrawn silence on one extreme to mischievous acting out on the other.

The student who has had a good deal of success in the past will be likely to risk success again; if he should fail, his self-concept can "afford" it. A student with a history predominated by failures will be reluctant to risk failure again. His depleted self-concept cannot afford it. Similar to someone living on a limited income, he will shop cautiously and look for bargains. One obvious recommendation in this situation is to make each learning step small enough so that the student is asked to only risk one chip at a time, instead of five. But even more obvious, in our eyes, is the need to build up the student's supply of poker chips so that he can begin to have a surplus of chips to risk.

If a student starts out, metaphorically speaking, with twenty chips and he gains fifteen more through the exercises contained in this book, then, even if he loses ten in a reading class, he is still five ahead of the game. But if he loses ten from a starting position of twenty he is now down to ten and in a very precarious psychological position. Viewed in this way, self-concept building can be seen as making sure that every student has enough chips to stay in the game.

In this book we offer you over 100 ways to build up each student's collection of chips![7]

---

[6] See William W. Purkey, *Self-Concept and School Achievement* (Englewood Cliffs, N.J.: Prentice-Hall, Inc., 1970), for a comprehensive review of the research.
[7] For a list of other materials currently available and workshops offered in the areas of humanistic education and self-concept development, write to the New England Center, Box 575, Amherst, Massachusetts 01002.

a note to teachers on how to use this book

WHEN TO USE THE EXERCISES

The question we are most asked by teachers who attend our workshops and classes is, "You know, I really think all of this is great, but with everything else I have to teach, where am I going to find time for this?" The practical experience of teachers who have used these materials indicates three general answers:

1. Many schools, recognizing the need for the holistic development of their students, have begun to inaugurate new courses, sometimes required and sometimes elective, with various titles such as Human Development, Education of the Self, Human Relations, Project Self, The Search for Self, Basic Communication, The Human Potential Program, etc. These classes explore various activities designed to help students understand and accept themselves better.

2. Where this is not possible because of rigid scheduling procedures, lack of budget, or lack of philosophical support on the part of the administration, another approach has worked well. This is to provide ten to twenty minutes every day or every other day to one or more of the exercises in the book. We usually suggest a heavier concentration during the first few weeks of school so that you can get things started off well, similar to the poker chip concept just mentioned. This regular ongoing activity can have a powerful effect on the classroom climate throughout the year. It can also provide the students with a cumulative, sequential, developmental curriculum in the affective domain—something sorely missing in our schools. It can also provide you with a greater feeling of excitement and energy as you experience what happens with your students. Our experience is that subject matter learning has never suffered because of time spent on self-concept building. Quite to the contrary, it seems to be enhanced with the new self-confidence of the students.

3. A third approach is to use the activities whenever you have some free time—a rainy day, a canceled field trip, a class when your scheduled movie doesn't arrive, a period when your lesson plan only takes half the expected time, a day when the students just don't seem to be with it, etc. Another good experience we've had with the materials is when we've had to

substitute for a sick teacher; rather than just having an extra study hall, we have used many of the exercises with a great deal of success and enjoyment.

HOW TO SEQUENCE THE ACTIVITIES

We have divided the activities into seven sections:

Getting Started
My Strengths
Who Am I?
Accepting My Body
Where Am I Going?
The Language of Self
Relationships with Others

The divisions seem to us to flow naturally one from the other. It is important to develop an environment of trust and support so that students will feel safe exploring themselves and interacting with each other (Part I). In order to begin to take risks and grow, they need to know where they are now and what their strengths are. They need to accept their present reality, including their bodies (Parts II, III, and IV). Then they need to have some sense of where they want to go, what they want to accomplish, and who they want to become (Part V). Part VI is devoted to understanding some of the ways children stop themselves from going where they want to go with their language. The last part is devoted to how students relate all of their emerging selves to others.

The activities within each section also have a natural sequence which will become apparent as you use them. However, we are not advocating that you use the exercises in the order they appear. Some are more appropriate for one age level than another, some may seem redundant, some too complex for the time you have available, and so on. Read through several of the exercises in each section. Get a feel for what is available here. Then think about your class for a minute. What is primary right now? How do you feel about the emotional and self-concept climate of your classroom? What activities seem like they would be fun to do? Which ones do you think your students would respond to? Put all this data together and make a choice. Try it out and see what happens. What next step seems to be indicated by the responses of the students? Try that out, and so on. After a while the process of choosing activities will become a natural one. You'll find that you will begin to understand the assumptions upon which the activities are based and then you'll be inventing exercises and activities of your own.

THE TEACHER'S ATTITUDE

Throughout the book we refer to "accepting the students' responses without judgment" or maintaining a "nonjudgmental attitude." By this we mean that when a student shares an experience, a reaction, a feeling, a thought, or whatever, we must accept it as a true expression of his reality, his existence, or his awareness at that point in time. We may not always agree with what someone else does or says; that is because we perceive reality differently, or perhaps we are more evolved in our awareness, our level of consciousness. Owing to our unique set of past experiences we may have come to hold different values than our students. And that's OK. That's who we are. The same is true of our students. That's who they are—unique individuals with differing views of themselves and their world. While we may be engaged in an endeavor to broaden their perceptions, heighten their awareness, and expand their consciousness, we must always respect their present state of being—which may be very different from ours.

If we are truly open to our students and accept them for who they are, then they too will begin to accept themselves as worthwhile beings—worthy of attention and love. There seems to be a natural and innate self-healing and self-actualizing process that occurs when one truly accepts oneself and the world as it is. Whole systems of psychology and many Eastern religious faiths are based on this single premise. We have observed the positive effects of such an approach in hundreds of classrooms with thousands of students.

We do not need to preach about "better ways of being" or moralize about how one *should* be. When we lecture students about themselves they tune us out, their defenses become stronger, and contact is blocked. We can ask them to examine the consequences of their behavior and to explore alternatives, but we have found that *it works better* to do this in the *nonjudgmental* spirit of broadening the student's options of choice rather than making him better because now he is somehow bad. This way of thinking may seem foreign to you. It is easy to get attached to a set of absolute values, but we do not intend to preach to you about a better way. Instead, we simply suggest you suspend your value judgments for a week or a day and see what happens. It has proved very valuable for us.

It is my conviction that education without self-knowledge in depth is a process which, like education itself, is never complete. It is a point on a continuous and never-ending journey. It is always relative, never absolute. It is a process which must go on throughout life, if at all; and like the fight for external freedom, it demands eternal vigilance and continuous struggle. This is because in every one of us, from the beginning of life until its end, active forces are at work which tend repeatedly to confuse and obscure our images of ourselves. Therefore, that well-known average man who lacks self-knowledge in depth looks out upon the world through glasses which are discolored by the quality of his own unconscious self-image. Without self-knowledge in depth we can have dreams, but no art. We can have the neurotic raw materials of literature but not mature literature. We can have no adults, but only aging children who are armed with words and paint and clay and atomic weapons, none of which they understand. And the greater the role in the educational process which is played by unconscious components of symbolic thinking, the wider must be this ancient and dishonorable gap between erudition and wisdom. It is this gap which makes a mockery of the more pretentious claims of art, of science, of education, and of religion.

Lawrence S. Kubie
Neurotic Distortion of the Creative Process

CHILDREN LEARN WHAT THEY LIVE

Dorothy Law Nolte

If a child lives with criticism,
    he learns to condemn.
If a child lives with hostility,
    he learns to fight.
If a child lives with fear,
    he learns to be apprehensive.
If a child lives with pity,
    he learns to feel sorry for himself.
If a child lives with ridicule,
    he learns to be shy.
If a child lives with jealousy,
    he learns what envy is.
If a child lives with shame,
    he learns to feel guilty.
If a child lives with encouragement,
    he learns to be confident.
If a child lives with tolerance,
    he learns to be patient.
If a child lives with praise,
    he learns to be appreciative.
If a child lives with acceptance,
    he learns to love.
If a child lives with approval,
    he learns to like himself.
If a child lives with recognition,
    he learns that it is good to have a goal.
If a child lives with sharing,
    he learns about generosity.
If a child lives with honesty and fairness,
    he learns what truth and justice are.
If a child lives with security,
    he learns to have faith in himself and in those about him.
If a child lives with friendliness,
    he learns that the world is a nice place in which to live.
If you live with serenity,
    your child will live with peace of mind.

        With what is your child living?

a note to parents

When we began writing this book, our first thought was of teachers. Teachers have immediate and daily contact with children and youth of all ages. The teacher-student relationship often lasts for several hours each day, so it seemed that the greatest opportunity for helping children to develp positive self-concepts and to learn to relate well with others lay in the schools. Being educators ourselves, classroom teachers seemed to be the logical target for our efforts.

As we began to test some of the exercises on our own children we realized the potential that lay in sharing our methods of development with parents. As our students and friends began to report the great success they had in using these activities with their children, we began to appreciate the influence parents could have in this area.

As teacher and principal we had experienced the frustration of attempting to teach kids whose self-concepts had been damaged by untrained and unskilled parents. Having had experience with hundreds of parents in teacher-parent meetings we also remembered that we had never once met a parent who didn't really want the best for his child. The motivation and the good intention were always there. What was lacking was the knowledge and the skills that make up good parenting. This book is by no means intended to be a comprehensive guide to parenting. There are many of those already available—some of which we have listed in the bibliography at the end of this book. We do feel, however, that the book provides a variety of ways to enhance the level of communication you have with your children, to learn more about each other, and to help your children develop a realistic and positive confidence in themselves.

YOU CAN DO IT

Any normal person can do the things suggested in *100 Ways*. You don't have to be a college graduate. You don't have to be a psychiatrist. You don't have to be emotionally superior. You do have to be able to read, of course, and have reasonable judgment and maturity, and be more sane than otherwise. It helps if you have a sense of humor, are fairly flexible, and if you operate democratically. These are qualities that enhance any relationship and certainly parent-child arrangements are no different. All our experience says, "Yes, go ahead! Try it!"

The key qualities of caring and empathy mean more in human relationships than any diplomas, degrees, or technical skills.

If you care enough about your children to be able to sense what they feel and perhaps even *feel* what they feel, you have all the prerequisites needed. So don't hesitate, with the guidance provided here, to use the material presented in this book to enrich your children's lives and your own life too!

DO IT WITH STYLE

We're going to be so bold as to suggest a specific mode in which to approach your children with these exercises: keep it light and make it fun!

Keep it Light

One of our college students often says, "Casual, man, Casual!" This is not bad advice at all. Let it happen when it happens. Don't force the exercises on your kids, and for heaven's sake don't make "lessons" out of them. When those moments occur when you have some time with your children, and the TV set is not on, and they're not distracted with other activities, simply begin an exercise as naturally as possible—perhaps saying something like, "Hey, I know something that would be fun" and just go ahead and do it. The exercise may be one you've kept in your head to try at the first opportunity or maybe it's one you've selected for a certain purpose with a particular child. In any event, be cool. Don't force participation when the kids are not interested. Another day may be quite a different story or another exercise might capture their attention. Remember, nothing you are going to accomplish in one day is worth risking possible bad feelings between you and your child.

Make It Fun

Light-hearted banter often accompanies this kind of "work," especially if four or five people are involved. Treat the activities as if they were games. Everyone plays including you. While a lot of fun and enjoyment are involved, these are also times for sharing and honesty. The times we engage in *100 Ways* are among our finest as a family. We parents invariably find ourselves talking later at night about the responses and reactions of our children to this or that exercise.

WHEN AND WHERE

We like to do these things whenever the opportunity presents itself. The real requirement is for a little time and not too much diversion. Trips in the car provide an excellent chance to talk; time can be passed in good spirited fun and children sense, as we do, that there is more to what we are discussing and experiencing than takes place in our usual day-to-day interactions. Over the years we've actually developed an expectation that we'll "play some of daddy's games" and all of us look forward to it.

When we eat dinner, whether at a restaurant or at home, we often find ourselves engaged in these sorts of activities. This particular time is so productive that two of our friends have written articles about the potential of the evening meal for learning and sharing.[1] There have also been many occasions when our guests and our families get into a fantasy or value clarification exercise because of an issue that has arisen in the conversation.

WHAT CAN YOU EXPECT?

If you try these activities you can expect to see some thinking going on—some really honest introspection. You can expect to see, every so slowly, some values beginning to develop. You can be certain that you are bringing to their awareness some feelings, attitudes, and beliefs that your children may not have been aware they possessed.

You can expect to have fun and to develop closer ties with your children. Often our interactions occur when one of the parents is alone with one of the children, and when that happens the warmth and love that is generated and renewed is beautiful to experience.

A word of caution in the midst of all our enthusiasm: don't expect a revolution! Overnight changes in your children's behavior are not likely. After all, it took a long time for them to get where they are, and it also takes time for the internalization of new ideas, new values, and new attitudes. But the process can be a growing experience for you and your children and that's what is really most important, isn't it? It is with great eagerness that we submit our book to you with the hope that the material here will make your life and your children's lives a little more meaningful and fulfilling.

---

[1] "Dinner Table Learning," by Sidney B. Simon, and "Clarify Values at the Family Table," by Howard Kirschenbaum. Both articles can be found in *Readings in Values Clarification* by Simon and Kirschenbaum (Minneapolis: Winston Press, 1973), pp. 265-70 and 272-79.

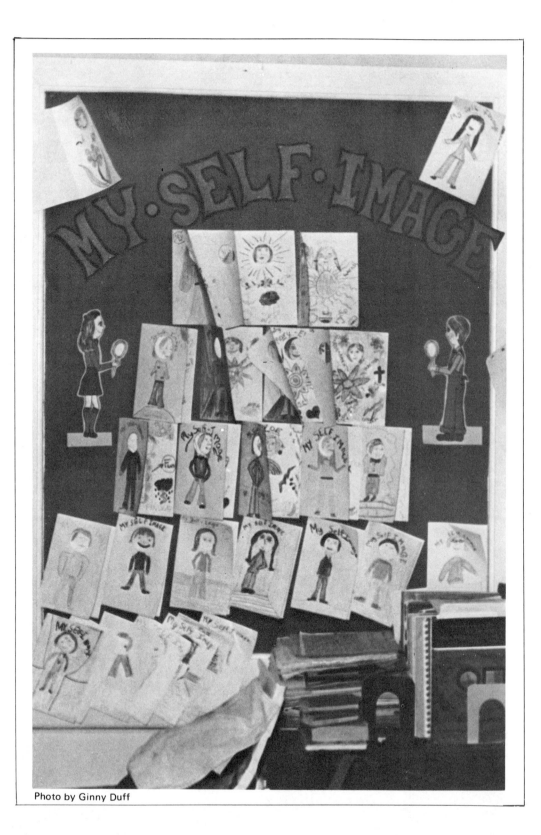

Photo by Ginny Duff

one
building
an environment
of positive support

As we said in the introduction, the exercises in this book will help you build a self-enhancing classroom climate. In part these start-up activities are designed for that purpose. They are simple, nonthreatening, and fun. They also begin the process of introspection, of getting into oneself to an extent not commonly experienced. They help the student become *aware* of himself in different dimensions. They indicate to him things in his life that make him proud. He sees that he surely has had some successes. He becomes aware of some of his deeper feelings and values. That this self-awareness is important is attested to by Rollo May:

> This growing awareness of one's body, wishes, and desires—processes, which are obviously related to the experiencing of identity—normally also bring heightened appreciation of one's self as a being and a heightened reverence for being itself.[1]

Besides beginning the task of creating a climate of positive support for class members and creating self-awareness, these activities contribute to the experience of one's identity—exactly as May mentioned above. The student begins to see himself as a distinct and unique individual.

This is an especially critical time in our history for this kind of education; the alienation of youth, the loss of identity (or, as Eric Erikson calls it, "the identity crisis") of so many young people has resulted in a severe social problem as well as an individual loss of potential.

The activities suggested here contribute to growth rather than alienation when used by sensitive and empathic teachers. Use the ones that seem most appropriate to you for your group. They can only lead to better lives for youngsters. They begin the process that leads to a feeling of "I'm OK!"

[1] *Love and Will* (New York: W. W. Norton & Company, Inc., 1969), p. 263.

LOVE AND THE CABBIE

Art Buchwald

I was in New York the other day and rode with a friend in a taxi. When we got out my friend said to the driver, "Thank you for the ride. You did a superb job of driving."

The taxi driver was stunned for a second. Then he said:

"Are you a wise guy or something?"

"No, my dear man, and I'm not putting you on. I admire the way you keep cool in heavy traffic."

"Yeh," the driver said and drove off.

"What was that all about?" I asked.

"I am trying to bring love back to New York," he said. "I believe it's the only thing that can save the city."

"How can one man save New York?"

"It's not one man. I believe I have made the taxi driver's day. Suppose he has 20 fares. He's going to be nice to those twenty fares because someone was nice to him. Those fares in turn will be kinder to their employees or shop-keepers or waiters or even their own families. Eventually the goodwill could spread to at least 1,000 people. Now that isn't bad, is it?"

"But you're depending on that taxi driver to pass your goodwill to others."

"I'm not depending on it," my friend said. "I'm aware that the system isn't foolproof so I might deal with 10 different people today. If, out of 10, I can make three happy, then eventually I can indirectly influence the attitudes of 3,000 more."

"It sounds good on paper," I admitted, "but I'm not sure it works in practice."

"Nothing is lost if it doesn't. I didn't take any of my time to tell that man he was doing a good job. He neither received a larger tip nor a smaller tip. If it fell on deaf ears, so what? Tomorrow there will be another taxi driver whom I can try to make happy."

"You're some kind of a nut," I said.

"That shows you how cynical you have become. I have made a study of this. The thing that seems to be lacking, besides money of course, for our postal employees, is that no one tells people who work for the post office what a good job they're doing."

"But they're not doing a good job."

"They're not doing a good job because they feel no one cares if they do or not. Why shouldn't someone say a kind word to them?"

We were walking past a structure in the process of being built and passed five workmen eating their lunch. My friend stopped. "That's a magnificent job you men have done. It must be difficult and dangerous work."

The five men eyed my friend suspiciously.

"When will it be finished?"

"June," a man grunted.

"Ah. That really is impressive. You must all be very proud."

We walked away. I said to him, "I haven't seen anyone like you since 'The Man from La Mancha.' "

"When those men digest my words, they will feel better for it. Somehow the city will benefit from their happiness."

"But you can't do this all alone!" I protested. "You're just one man."

"The most important thing is not to get discouraged. Making people in the city become kind again is not an easy job, but if I can enlist other people in my campaign. . ."

"You just winked at a very plain looking woman," I said.

"Yes, I know," he replied. "And if she's a schoolteacher, her class will be in for a fantastic day."

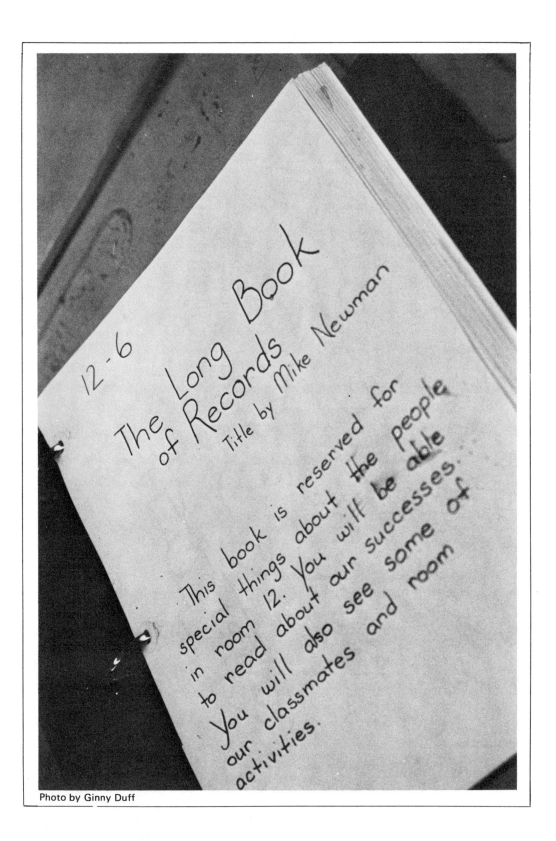

Photo by Ginny Duff

1

the journal

One way to most profitably use the exercises presented in this book is to have the students keep a journal of their reactions (feelings, thoughts, behaviors, "I learned. . ." statements, etc.) to each activity. Keeping a journal has several advantages. It allows the student to keep an ongoing account of how he is growing, of what is happening to him,* of how he uniquely responds to a given situation. It provides a cumulative statement of who he is, how he sees himself, and how others see him.

The more a person learns about himself, the more he will expand his concept of himself. Many times what is learned in an exercise is overlooked if it is not explicitly stated. Dr. Sidney B. Simon suggests that students make what he calls "I learned. . ." statements. After each activity, ask the students to record what they have learned *about themselves* in the form of "I learned. . ." statements:

> I learned that I. . .
> I relearned that I. . .
> I was surprised to find that I. . .
> I reaffirmed that I. . .

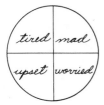

I am mad that my brother punched me and hurt my arm on the way to school. I am worried that he'll do it again on the way home.

---

*We have struggled long and hard in relation to the words *him* and *her, he* and *she*, etc. For a while we attempted him/her, but it became too cumbersome. We hope you will understand our situation and know that we are aware of the problems in female self-concept as related to our language structure. We have not yet found a satisfactory substitution. We welcome any suggestions.

These can be included in the students' journals sometimes and on other occasions worked into a class discussion.

We have found it useful when working with students in the affective domain to precede and follow each activity with a "here and now wheel." Ask the students to draw a circle with four lines intersecting in it at right angles (see below). On the lines have the students write one word that describes how they are feeling right now (i.e., happy, sad, tired, frustrated, anxious, relaxed, angry, loving, stupid, foolish, confident, etc.). Then ask them to choose one of the four words and expand it into two sentences. For example, "I feel happy because Sally picked me to be her partner. I didn't know she liked me."

Having the students compare their wheels before and after an exercise helps them see how their feelings about themselves change during an activity.

It is the cumulative effect over a long period of time that makes the journal effective. As it evolves into a very complete book about the student, it will become a precious document to him.

the journal—
a beginning

Writing an autobiography is a good exercise for juniors and seniors in high school, especially for an English class. One way to approach such an effort is to break the task into smaller components. The exercises that appear below can all be done as individual writing assignments in preparation for writing an autobiography. These assignments can be written in individual journals.

1. Ask students to write an autobiography of their hair. It is to be written as if their hair were the author. They should describe all the major events and changes in their lives as their hair.

2. Have the students draw the floor plans of the last two apartments or houses they have lived in. When they have completed their drawings, ask them to form into groups of three. Ask them to take the other members of their group on a guided tour through one of their houses, describing all the rooms, the furniture in them, where they used to play, study, hide, watch TV, sleep, eat, day-dream, etc. When working with college students or teacher trainees, have them draw floor plans of their elementary or high school.

3. Ask the students to list who their heroes or heroines were when they were in elementary and junior high schools. Who were the bullies in their neighborhood? Who were their friends?

4. Who has been most influential in shaping their lives to date?

5. Have them write about the special events of their lives—both good and bad. How did they affect them when they occurred? How do they affect them now?

Life is nothing but wasted time
To those who don't enjoy it.
Oh, if man were like animals
Instead of thinking the worst
War, poverty, slavery and tragedies.

Man is such a queer animal!
His mind thinks oddly
Upon the past tragedies.
The good times are wiped away
Far away, when we recall our life.

Charles Finnegan, Grade 5, 1970
Katherine Lee Bates School, Wellesley, Massachusetts

"I have blue eyes and dark brown hair. I have some freckles, not many though. I have a small nose. I have regular size ears. I have medium size hair."

Lawrence Branagan and Christopher Moroney

3
autobiographical
questionnaires

The autobiographical questionnaire is another tool to help a student expand his perception of himself. Looked at from semester to semester, the questionnaire can be an important instrument in helping someone enhance his self-concept.

At the beginning of each semester and again at the end of the year, the students should be asked to fill out the questionnaire. Having the students review their answers at the end of the year is a very illuminating experience in the quest for answers to the question "Who am I?"

Listed below are some sample questions for an autobiographical questionnaire. You should feel free to delete, add, or adapt questions from this list in order to fit your particular needs.

1. Name
2. Birth date   Age in years
3. Address   Phone number
4. List ten words that best describe you.
5. List ten words that best describe each person in your family.
6. What do you see yourself doing five years from now? Ten years from now? Twenty?
7. How do you spend your time after school and on weekends?
8. Of all the things you do in your free time, which do you like the most? The least?
9. Without mentioning specific names, what are the qualities of adults you respect and admire the most? The least? What are you doing to become more like the former? To keep from being like the latter?
10. Who is your best friend? What do your friends have in common?
11. What are your favorite sports, hobbies, or crafts, if any?
12. What are your favorite TV shows?
13. What magazines do you enjoy reading regularly?
14. What is there about you that makes your friends like you?
15. What major goals are you working on right now?
16. What does friendship mean to you?

17. What do you think of school?
18. Are you content with yourself? Would you like to be better? Would you like help and advice in this respect?
19. What value has life for you?
20. How do you spend your free time?

Adapted from Sidney B. Simon

> *A child's life is like a piece of paper on which every passerby leaves a mark.*
>
> Ancient Chinese proverb

PERSONAL TIME LINE FROM EXERCISE 4

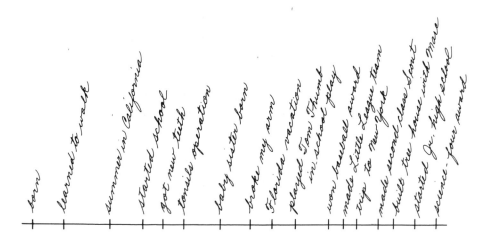

4
PERSONAL TIME LINE

The time line can serve as a substitute for, or a preliminary outline to, an autobiography. Begin with a discussion of the many different personal experiences that make up individual lives. Encourage students to recall significant events that influenced or affected their own lives—experiences that, at the time, involved their feelings and attitudes about themselves. Then have the students record the events—both positive and negative—along either side of a vertical line which represents their individual life span from birth to the present.

Draw a horizontal line in the center of a piece of legal-sized paper (or any other long paper) in pencil or ink. The line should extend from about one inch above the bottom edge to two inches from the top—allowing space for the title and the student's name.

Beginning at the left, with birth, work along the line to the present time. Strict chronology is not important. It may be necessary to stimulate the class's thinking by indicating some of the more common experiences, such as learning to talk and walk, starting school, childhood diseases, travel, special gifts, injuries, hospitalization, illnesses, getting glasses, Boy and Girl Scouts, Little League, losing pets, deaths of relatives, new brothers and sisters, etc.

Completed time lines could be placed in the students' journals or displayed with personal collages or self-portraits.

From the *Handbook for the Human Relations Approach to Teaching,*
Human Relations Education Center of the Buffalo Public Schools,
James J. Foley, Director

Man's self-concept is enhanced when he takes responsibility for himself.

William C. Shutz
Here Comes Everybody

5

the life line

The Life Line is an outgrowth of the Personal Time Line. A long piece of heavy yarn or string represents each individual's life. One end is birth, the other death. Using 3 × 5 index cards and paper clips, students decorate the yarn with the important events of their past and project what they think will happen in the future.

The value of this activity lies with the opportunity to display and discuss each life line.

From the *Handbook for the Human Relations Approach to Teaching,*
Human Relations Education Center of the Buffalo Public Schools,
James J. Foley, Director

For men and women are not only themselves; they are also the region in which they were born, the city apartment or farm in which they learned to walk, the games they played as children, the old wives' tales they overheard, the food they ate, the schools they attended, the sports they followed, the poems they read, and the God they believed in.

W. Somerset Maugham
The Razor's Edge

"What did I invent? I'm Gregory Phillips Wallingford.
I invented names."

Saturday Review, October 31, 1970

6

the name game

This two-part exercise has several learning goals. It can be used to help students learn each other's names and to establish positive feelings of the students toward themselves and toward their classmates. In the event that the students are already well acquainted, start with Part Two.

1. The class sits in a circle. The teacher starts by saying, "I am Miss Jones."* The first student to her right says, "I am Billy and that's Miss Jones." This process is continued around the circle until the last person has repeated everybody's name.

2. The second time around, each person must add something he is good at in addition to his name. For example, "I am singing Miss Jones." "I am basketball-playing Billy and that's singing Miss Jones." "I am mountain-climbing Sally and that's basketball-playing Billy and that's singing Miss Jones." And so on around the circle.

3. Another variation is to have each person add an adjective that describes how he is feeling at the moment. For example, "I'm happy Miss Jones." "I'm tired Billy and that's happy Miss Jones." "I'm angry Sally and that's tired Billy and that's happy Miss Jones."

> *In all things we learn only from those we love.*
>
> Goethe

> *The teacher gives not of his wisdom, But rather of his faith and lovingness.*
>
> *The Prophet*
> Kahlil Gibran

---

*We are believers in giving students the option to call teachers by their first names, too, if they want to. For instance, when we teach—even elementary grades—we tell the children they can call us Jack and Harold or Mr. Canfield and Dr. Wells. Some feel comfortable on a first-name basis; others don't. The idea is not to get locked into "shoulds." You might ask yourself, "How much of my self-concept is attached to what I'm called?" One teacher we know experimented for a day, having all the students call her Connie—and she called them Mr. _____ and Miss _____. The results were quite interesting. We feel that the approved use of first names helps establish a mutual and more equal feeling of rapport in the classroom. However, we realize that not all teachers are comfortable being addressed by their first name; they may feel it indicates a lack of respect. If your kids now call you Mr., Mrs., or Ms. try the above experiment, and at the end of the class or at the end of the day, talk about how you and the students felt. What was different about it? Did you like it? Were you uncomfortable?

7

one special thing

This exercise is a good one to use early in the semester because it helps to build a sense of group rapport through the establishment of an environment for self-disclosure.

Divide the class into pairs. Instruct the students to carry on a normal conversation for five minutes, each person telling the other as much as possible about himself. Ask the students to pick those things about themselves that they think are important to share.

After five minutes ask the class to come back together again as one large group (preferably in a circle). Then ask each student to introduce his partner by stating his partner's name and the one special thing that impressed him as most important about that person.

If you like, you can end the discussion by asking the group to talk about what it was like to talk to the other person and what it was like to be talked about in the group.

> *Every person needs recognition. It is expressed cogently by the lad who says, "Mother, let's play darts. I'll throw the darts and you say 'Wonderful.'"*
> *Educator's Handbook of Stories, Quotes, and Humor*
> M. Dale Baughman

8

autobiographical sharing

In order for the child's self-concept to grow, he needs to be in an environment of trust and support so that he can feel secure enough to take risks. One of the best methods for developing an environment of trust is mutual self-disclosure.

Ask the students to sit in a circle. Tell them that each of them will have a specific amount of time in which to give an autobiographical sketch. Appoint one student with a second hand on his watch to be the timer. If you're working with elementary students, you may have to supply the watch. When working with a small group of eight to ten students, you may wish to use a three-minute egg timer.

Ask the students to share those important experiences throughout their lives, beginning with early childhood, which they consider of importance in the sense of leaving a strong impression on their personalities.

In this type of exercise it is a good idea for you to be the first one to share in order to model the behavior you want from the students. This also creates an environment of less risk. After you have shared, you may want to flip a coin to decide whether to proceed clockwise or counterclockwise around the circle.

After sharing the autobiographical sketches, you can ask the students if they would like to go around again and share things they remembered as the others were talking. Perhaps you or the students would like to suggest other areas for sharing. One fourth-grade class we worked with decided that they wanted to share accounts of their past physical injuries.

As you facilitate the sharing, take advantage of opportunities to point out commonalities in the experiences of the students; i.e., "Wow, we sure have a lot of ex-Girl Scouts in this group, don't we?" "Gee, Bill! Did you and John know that you both played drums?"

Adapted from Herbert A. Otto

Joy is the feeling that comes from the fulfillment of one's potential. Fulfillment brings to an individual the feeling that he can cope with his environment; the sense of confidence in himself as a significant, competent, lovable person who is capable of handling situations as they arise, able to use fully his own capacities, and free to express his feelings.   *Joy*

William C. Schutz

"Guess who Miss Price picked to play poison ivy in the class play."

Chon Day; © 1970 by Saturday Review, Inc. SR/May 2, 1970

9

GUESS WHO I AM?

This can be used as a get-acquainted activity or a getting-to-know-you activity later in the year. It focuses everyone's attention on one person in a healthy way and gives that person a moment in the spotlight.

Have your students write out some biographical information that describes them but does not make it too obvious who they are. Include such things as hobbies, talents, major trips they have taken, unusual things about their family, and so on.

When each person has done this, collect the cards and read them while the class attempts to guess who is being described.

Include a card of your own!

> *I am* somebody! *I may be poor—but I am* somebody! *I may be in prison—but I am* somebody! *I may be uneducated—but I am* somebody!
>
> Rev. Jesse Jackson

10

getting to know you

Getting to know another person can be an exciting adventure. One of the most important aspects of getting to know another person is the exchange of information. In fact, one of the causes of problems in a relationships is the simple lack of information. When you don't know something about someone, you tend to fill in the vacuum with assumptions, fantasies, and unrealistic expectations. As we begin to know another person, it is important to get some of our "who" and "why" and "what" questions answered.

We have listed below a series of questions that can be used in several different ways. Students can be asked to pick a partner and answer some or all of these questions. You could give them the entire list on a duplicated sheet, write it on the blackboard, or just use a few of the questions. You can also have students pick a partner, answer one or two questions chosen by you, and then pick another partner, and so on. This way each person gets to know a little more about a lot of other people. You could also use these questions in small groups of four to six students.

The questions listed below work best with teenagers and adults.

1. How would your parents have described you as a child (age 6 to 12)?
2. What was your favorite toy as a child?
3. What is your favorite toy now?
4. What were you most proud of as a child?
5. What was your childhood nickname and how did you feel about it?
6. Do you like your first name now? If not, what would you like instead?
7. What is your favorite possession?
8. Can you name a favorite possession you no longer possess, and describe your feelings about no longer having it?
9. What is the funniest thing that ever happened to you?
10. What is the silliest thing you have ever done?
11. What is the stupidest thing you have ever done?
12. What is your all-time favorite movie? Why does it have special meaning for you?
13. What is your favorite book? What in it has personal meaning for you?

14. With what fictional hero or heroine do you most closely identify?
15. How good a friend are you? Give an example.
16. With what member of your family do you most identify? Why?
17. If you had to be someone else instead of yourself, whom would you choose? Why?
18. Who is your best friend of the same sex?
19. Who is your best friend of the opposite sex?
20. What do you look for most in a friend?
21. Name something you hate to do. What do you hate about it?
22. What in life is most important to you?
23. What do you like most about this class?
24. What do you like least about this class?
25. How would you change this class to make it better?

This exercise was adapted from the work of Jerry Gillies.
We recommend his book *My Needs, Your Needs, Our Needs* (New York: Doubleday, 1974).
Written primarily for couples, the exercises and concepts are easily adapted to any relationship,
such as the teacher-student or student-student relationship.

> *The secret of education lies in respecting the pupil.*
> Ralph Waldo Emerson
> *The Complete Works of Ralph Waldo Emerson*

11
success fantasy

Guided fantasy is a technique that is extremely useful and has become increasingly popular in recent years in various kinds of therapy. This particular fantasy is easy, fun, and nonthreatening. A good warm-up for the next activity—Success Sharing.

Ask the students to close their eyes. Suggest that they open and close them several times in order to become comfortable having them closed. Ask them to imagine that there is a motion picture screen in front of their eyes and that they can recall their past and project it onto the screen.

Have them think back to a really happy day when they were between six and ten years of age. Ask them to see themselves waking up in the bedroom they slept in at that time. Can they remember whether they had a single, twin, bunk bed, or couch? Did they share the room with anyone? The bed? Ask them to look around the room and see the other furniture. Where were their toys kept? Was there a window? Did they have breakfast first, go to the bathroom, wash up, play with their pet, or what? Ask them to imagine a typical day—their school, their playmates, their playground, etc.

Ask them, with their eyes still closed, to begin to focus on a success they had during that period of their life. Can they remember one? Where did it take place? Did they do it alone? Did they plan for it or did it happen spontaneously? Can they remember how it felt when they completed the achievement? Can they recreate those feelings in their bodies now? Did they tell anyone about the success? Whom? Can they remember that experience? How did that person, or those people, react? etc.

Have them open their eyes and share their success experiences with the group.

> *From Freud we learned that the past exists now in the person. Now we must learn, from growth theory and self-actualization theory, that the future also now exists in the person in the form of ideals, hopes, goals, unrealized potentials, mission, fate, destiny, etc. One for whom no future exists is reduced to the concrete, to helplessness, to emptiness. For him, time must be endlessly "filled." Striving, the usual organizer of most activity, when lost, leaves the person unorganized and unintegrated.*
>
> Abraham H. Maslow
> *Perceiving, Behaving, Becoming*

taking a positive look

One of the first steps to a more successful life is to stop dwelling on the negative past—one's mistakes and failures. Instead, a person should explore and build upon his successes and achievements, thus evolving a positive attitude rather than a negative one.

Most people restrict the use of their own potentialities. We are taught, throughout our lives certain attitudes that limit our growth and effectiveness. These attitudes are taught in our homes, our schools, and most of our formal religious institutions. These attitudes were pointed out extremely well in a conversation between Alice and the Mad Hatter in Wonderland.

Alice: Where I come from, people study what they are *not* [emphasis **added**] good at in order to be able to do what they *are* good at.

Mad Hatter: We only go around in circles in Wonderland; but we always end up where we started. Would you mind explaining yourself?

Alice: Well, grown-ups tell us to find out what we did wrong, and never do it again.

Mad Hatter: That's odd! It seems to me that in order to find out about something you have to study it. And when you study it, you should become better at it. Why should you want to become better at something and then never do it again? But please continue.

Alice: Nobody ever tells us to study the right things we do. We're only supposed to learn from the wrong things. But we are permitted to study the right things *other* people do. And sometimes we're even told to copy them.

Mad Hatter: That's cheating!

Alice: You're quite right, Mr. Hatter. I do live in a topsy-turvy world. It seems like I have to do something wrong first, in order to learn from that what not to do. And then, by not doing what I'm not supposed to do, perhaps I'll be right. But I'd rather be right the first time, wouldn't you?

Lewis Carroll
Alice in Wonderland

John Tenniel; Clarkson N. Potter, Inc.

12

success sharing

Another way to help students focus on the positive aspects of themselves is to have them publicly share their accomplishments with the group.

In small groups of five or six, or with the entire class, ask the students to share a success, accomplishment, or achievement they had before they were ten years old. Next ask them to share a success they had between the ages of ten and fifteen; then between the ages of fifteen to the present time. (Obviously, these age ranges will need to be revised depending upon the ages of the students in your class.)

At first some students may have difficulty remembering some of their earlier successes, but as others share theirs, they will recall their own. Children with extremely low self-concepts often report that they haven't had any successes. If this happens, you will need to help prod the students with questions such as:

> Well, you've been taking care of your younger brothers and sisters for two years; I consider that an accomplishment!
> Can you remember when you learned to ride your bicycle? Did you feel good about that achievement?

One way to enrich the effect of this exercise is to precede it with the Success Fantasy (see Exercise 11).

A variation of this exercise is to periodically ask your students to share their greatest success or accomplishment during a recent period of time—say, the past week, the last month, over the weekend, over vacation break, over the summer, etc. It is also a good practice at the end of each day to ask the students what their greatest success was for the day (see Exercise 17).

> *. . . over time, a continuing and steadfast focus on the positive in life, on our strengths, and on the strengths of others can help to restore in our students their personal energy, their feelings of power, their sense of worth so that they can see themselves as positive forces who can contribute to the task of building a better world.*
>
> Robert C. Hawley
> *Human Values in the Classroom*

13

the magic box

This is an excellent exercise for elementary school children.

Construct a "magic box" which can be any kind of a box with a mirror placed so as to reflect the face of anyone who looks inside. Begin the activity by asking the class, "Who do you think is the most special person in the whole world?" After allowing the children to respond with their individual answers, you may then continue, "Well, I have a magic box with me today, and each of you will have a chance to look inside and discover the most important person in the world."

Give each child a chance to look into the box after you ask them who they think they will see. Some children may have to be coaxed, because they may not believe what they see. Be ready with some of the following comments: "Are you surprised?" "How does it feel to see that you are the special person?" "You smiled so big—like you're happy to see that you're the special person." Before rejoining the class, ask each child to keep the special news a secret.

After all the children have had their turns, ask the group who the most special person was. After each child has had an opportunity to say "me," explain that the box is valuable because it shows that each of them is a special person. You might then want to ask how it is possible for everyone to be the special one. A discussion about each individual's uniqueness may ensue.

Suggested by Marlowe Berg, California State University at San Diego
and Patricia Wolleat, University of Wisconsin

Whenever a value is set forth which can only be attained by a few, the conditions are ripe for widespread feelings of personal inadequacy. An outstanding example in American society is the fierce competitiveness of the school system. No educational system in the world has so many examinations, or so emphasizes grades, as the American school system. Children are constantly being ranked and evaluated. The superior achievement of one child tends to debase the achievement of another.

Morris Rosenberg

Society and the Adolescent Self-Image

14
BRAGGING

We have found that bragging is a more informal variation of the Pride Line (Exercise 16) and success-sharing exercises that work well with high school and college students.

Ask the students to form groups of five or six members. Tell them that each person has five minutes to boast about anything he feels like in his life: accomplishments, awards, skills, things he does well, personal characteristics, etc.

This activity usually results in everybody feeling very good about himself, as well as creating a heightened sense of group rapport.

It is important to receive recognition and positive support for what one does. Exercises such as the Pride Line, success sharing, and bragging provide a legitimate forum for disclosing those things about one's self that are positive and growth-promoting. If a person is to become fully self-actualizing, it is important for him to learn to express his positive as well as his negative feelings. However, our society does not provide much opportunity for this; bragging is generally frowned upon. Look at all the "put-downs" that are commonly used in regard to bragging:

> He's really a *stuffed shirt.*
> If his *head gets any bigger,* he won't be able to wear a hat.
> She's the most *self-centered* person I know.
> He's always *blowing his own horn.*
> With all your bragging, you need to get a *press agent.*
> There he goes again—always *beating his own drum.*

You may wish to ask the students to share whatever feelings they have about the bragging they just did. Were they uncomfortable bragging? Listening to others brag? Did they feel that their stories were less spectacular than those of the others? Were there any particular people whose stories they resented or admired?

We learned this from Emily Coleman.

Until I accept my faults I will most certainly doubt my virtues.

Hugh Prather
Notes to Myself

Paul Peter Porges; © 1971 by Saturday Review/World

15
mirror bragging

A variation of the previous exercise can be used to help people become more aware of how they tend to disown the part of themselves that wants to brag and tell people how great they are. Unfortunately, most people imagine that if they talk positively about themselves, others will reject them. It is true that some people become obnoxious bores with their never-ending tales of achievement and greatness, but they represent the extreme. By never talking positively about themselves, many people end up *deadening* a very natural part of their being.

For this exercise ask each student to find a partner—someone he trusts. Then ask one person to designate himself as "A" and the other as "B." Instruct the "A's" to spend the next several minutes "bragging" about some aspect of their life—an achievement, a skill they possess, etc. The "B's" are to sit directly opposite their partners and act as "mirrors," i.e., to imitate every aspect of "A"—posture, body movements, and facial gestures— as they brag. This gives the "A's" an opportunity to see how they come across as braggers.

When two minutes have elapsed, instruct the "B's" to give the "A's" feedback about how they experienced them as braggarts. Then allow the "A's" to respond with how they experienced themselves during the exercise. After a while, roles should be switched and the exercise repeated.

Most people feel uncomfortable bragging. The usual cause of the discomfort is an imagined fear of rejection for being too self-centered. Another fear often expressed is "If I brag about myself, you may find out I'm really not that good and try to make a fool of me." As a result of this fear, many people squelch their spontaneous good feelings about themselves.

As a final step, ask the students to repeat the exercise, this time exaggerating by standing up proudly, throwing chests out, talking enthusiastically, etc. The results should then be compared again.

I yam what I yam and that's all that I yam.

Popeye the Sailor Man

16
pride line

Pride is related to self-concept. People enjoy expressing pride in something they've done that might have gone unrecognized otherwise. Our culture does not encourage such expressions and it is sometimes difficult for people to actually say, "I'm proud that I. . ."

Ask each student to make a statement about a specific area of behavior, beginning with, "I'm proud that I. . ." For example, you might say, "I'd like you to mention something about your *letter writing* that you're proud of. Please begin your response with 'I am proud that I. . .' " Students may pass if they wish.

Below are some suggested items for use in this exercise.

1. Things you've done for your parents
2. Things you've done for a friend
3. Work in school
4. How you spend your free time
5. About your religious beliefs
6. How you've earned some money
7. Something you've bought recently
8. How you usually spend your money
9. Habits you have
10. Something you do often
11. What you are proudest of in your life
12. Something you have shared
13. Something you tried hard for
14. Something you own
15. Thoughts about people who are different from you
16. Something you've done in regard to ecology
17. Something you've done in regard to racism

We learned this exercise from our friend Sid Simon.
We highly recommended his very useful book,
co-authored with Leland W. Howe and Howard Kirschenbaum,
Values Clarification: A Handbook of Practical Strategies for Teachers and Students
(New York: Hart Publishing Co., 1972).

Self love, my liege, is not so vile a sin as self neglecting.

Shakespeare
King Henry V, act II, scene 4

Don Rutledge from Black Star

17
success a day

At the end of each day, have the students briefly share with the rest of the class the successes they have experienced during that day.

Some students will find this difficult at first, but as others begin to share, they too will realize they have had some of the same successes. It has been our experience that if a student says he has had no success, some of his classmates will chime in with successes they have seen him accomplish. The sensitive teacher will also look for successes to be pointed out to the child with extremely low self-esteem.

A variation of this activity is to have each child share with the class what he feels he has learned that day. In addition to being a great form of review, it provides the student with a sense of accomplishment. Without recall, students are often not consciously aware of all the learning they are accomplishing in and out of school each day. Knowing that he is learning adds positively to a child's self-concept.

If you are trying to build writing skills, have the students write a paragraph recording their successes rather than reporting them verbally. This method also leaves an accumulated record which the student can review at the end of the week.

True, all children need to experience their competence to build self-respect. But each child needs to feel that his person is cherished regardless of his competence. Successful performances build the sense of worthwhileness; being cherished as a person nurtures the feeling of being loved. Every child needs to feel both *loved and worthwhile. But* lovability must not be tied to worthwhile performance. *The more lovable any child feels, however, the more likely he is to perform in satisfactory ways, for then he likes himself.*

Dorothy Corkille Briggs
Your Child's Self-Esteem

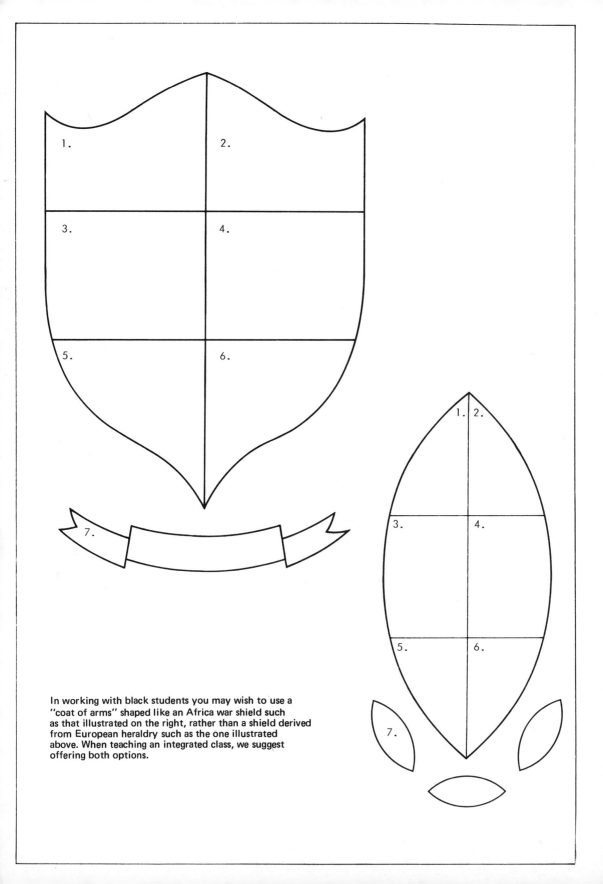

In working with black students you may wish to use a "coat of arms" shaped like an Africa war shield such as that illustrated on the right, rather than a shield derived from European heraldry such as the one illustrated above. When teaching an integrated class, we suggest offering both options.

18

PERSONAL COAT OF ARMS

This exercise is a way of combining several self-enhancing questions with some art work and small group disclosure.

Print up ditto sheets with the design that appears on the opposite page and distribute it to the students. Ask each of them to create an individual coat of arms by making a drawing in the appropriate section expressing their thoughts regarding each of the following questions:

1. Express in a drawing the most significant event in your life from birth to age fourteen.
2. Express in a drawing the most significant event in your life from age fourteen to the present.
3. Express in a drawing your greatest success or achievement in the past year.
4. Express in a drawing your happiest moment in the past year.
5. If you had one year to live and were guaranteed success in whatever you attempted, what would you attempt? Draw a picture expressing your answer.
6. Express in a drawing something you are good at.
7. If you died today, what three words would you most like to be said of you?

Any number of questions could be substituted for those above in order to adapt the exercise to different age levels. Some optional questions for drawings are:

1. What is something you are striving to become or be?
2. What is your family's greatest achievement?
3. What would you want to accomplish by the time you are sixty-five?
4. Draw a picture of something you'd like to become better at.

When the drawings are completed, ask the students to form groups of five or six and share what they have done with the small group. When they have finished sharing, you may wish to post all the coats of arms on a bulletin board or wall for a day or two.

After the students have shared their drawings in the small groups, you may wish to have them make several "I learned. . ." statements in their journals.

Suggested by Sister Louise, St. Juliana's School, Chicago, Illinois

19

personal flag

The teacher begins this activity by holding up a symbol (e.g., the peace symbol) and asks if anyone knows what it is. He may then respond with, "Yes, it is a peace symbol. It's a popular symbol that many people recognize. I have some other symbols with me also. Look at this one and see if you can tell what it means." The teacher may then hold up a dollar sign, for example. "Here are some other symbols [mathematical symbols, traffic symbols, etc.] that you probably see every day. Can you think of others?"

The teacher should then explain that a symbol is a picture or design that stands for something, just as the peace symbol represents the idea of peace. "People make symbols. Someone makes up the symbol and the rest of us learn what it means. Let's see if we can make up some of our own." The children can then work as a group in making up symbols for such concepts as happiness, spring, sadness, family, sports, etc.

The teacher may then show a picture of an American flag and explain that a flag is another kind of symbol and consists of many parts. "Does anyone know what the stars stand for? the stripes? the colors? Every country has a flag and the different parts of the flag stand for something that is important to the people. Today you are going to make your own *personal* flags, and make symbols for things about *you*."

The personal flag may be used as a way of identifying symbols of feeling toward a variety of people and situations—e.g., friendship, school, careers, special moments, values, habits, life goals, etc.

After the children have completed their drawings the teacher can then lead a discussion in which the students are asked to share the meanings of their symbols with the rest of the class if they wish. At this point it is important for the teacher to keep in mind that it is not his task to give advice to the children, but rather to show interest and understanding and reflect on the value and meaning of their symbolized experiences.

Suggested by Marlowe Berg and Patricia Wolleat.

Perhaps the most important single cause of a person's success or failure educationally has to do with the question of what he believes about himself.

Arthur W. Combs

Perceiving, Behaving, and Becoming

20

collage of self

Instruct your students to make a collage entitled "Me!" Provide each student with a 12 X 18-inch sheet of thick construction paper or thin cardboard. They should collect and cut out pictures, words, and symbols that are representative of themselves—things they like to do, things they own, things they would like to own, places they've been, people they admire, etc. Then they are to paste these pictures, words, and symbols onto their sheets of construction paper to make a collage. Instruct the students not to sign them.

After the individual collages are completed, display them in the classroom. First, have the students try to guess who made each collage. Next have each student explain to the class all the items in his collage. Note for the class that the collages are all somewhat different—unique—just as each person, while having much in common with all others, is a different and unique individual.

You will probably need several class periods to complete this project. Try to have a lot of magazines with pictures available for the students. Magazines such as *Ms., Ebony, Black Sports, Women in Sports, Auto World,* etc., should be included. The greater the variety of magazines, the better.

Caterpillar: . . . and who are you?

Alice: I . . . I hardly know, Sir, just at present—at least I know who I was when I got up this morning, but I think I must have changed several times since then.

Lewis Carroll
Alice in Wonderland

Photo by Ginny Duff

21

self-portrait

This is a good initial activity for any age level. The self-portrait can be easily and effectively executed as a sketch, drawing or painting in a wide variety of art media, such as chalk, pencil, ink, charcoal, crayon, pastel, water color or tempera. Length of the activity will be largely determined by age level and the particular medium selected.

Self-portraits may be created impromptu from memory or from mirrors. Be accepting and encouraging during the pupil's first try; wait a few weeks—then try again. It is helpful if you work along with the class on a portrait of yourself. In fact, teacher participation is suggested for all of the activities in this book.

Create occasions for displaying the self-portraits frequently. Birthdays and special projects provide ideal opportunities for using portraits. Try using signed portraits in place of name tags to identify individual students' projects and papers.

From the *Handbook for the Human Relations Approach to Teaehing*, Human Relations Education Center of the Buffalo Public Schools, James J. Foley. Director.

Oliver Wendell Holmes once attended a meeting in which he was the shortest man present.
"Doctor Holmes," quipped a friend, "I should think you'd feel rather small among us big fellows."
"I do," retorted Holmes, "I feel like a dime among a lot of pennies."

UPI Photo

22

success symbols

All of us have symbols of success—things that remind us of our past successes. We have photographs, medals, certificates, dried-up corsages, dance books, ticket stubs, autographed baseballs, newspaper clippings, poetry, bronzed shoes, trophies, plaques, ribbons, and mounted golf balls, fish, and antlers. Most of us save these objects because they remind us of our abilities and competencies and our likability and popularity.

Have the students bring to class five tangible objects that recall or symbolize some past successes or accomplishments they have had.

During the next class period have each student share one or more of his "success symbols" with the rest of the class. Instruct the students to share the feelings and meaning connected with the specific object as well as the success it symbolizes.

A variation of the success symbol concept is to have the students list five success symbols they do not have but would like to acquire in the next year, five years; etc. This activity could be used in conjunction with goal-setting. Be sure to discuss the choices or goals without judgment; be open to whatever the students come up with.

As a teacher, what are your success symbols? Take a walk through your house or apartment and see how many are visible. If they are all stored away in drawers and closets, consider how you might make them a more *integral* part of your environment.

Suggested by Herbert Otto
in *A Guide to Developing Your Potential* (New York: Charles Scribner's Sons, 1967).

A first-grader proudly showed his mother the gold star he had earned in school. "We get these for what we do best," he explained. "And what do you do best?" she asked. "I'm the best rester!" beamed the boy.
Everyone wants to be good at something. And most of us are. Young, old, or middle-aged, we all have a built-in drive to excel.

23

WHAT'S MY BAG?

Combine the previous Exercises 20 and 22. Have the students collect a large number of success symbols and other meaningful objects that represent who they are and place them in a shopping bag.

Next, have them decorate the outside of the shopping bag with personally related pictures, words, and symbols, thus producing a three-dimensional collage.

This exercise can also be done using a cigar box or any other kind of container.

> *The child must first learn self-respect and a sense of dignity that grows out of his increasing self-understanding before he can learn to respect the personalities and rights and differences of others.*
>
> Virginia M. Axline
> *Dibs: In Search of Self*

24

social silhouettes

Before embarking on this project, talk with the class about how easy it is to cut someone down, to criticize, and to belittle. Discuss the fact that there is much good in others that can be found if we look. This project involves looking at one another, seeing the good, and telling the other person about it.

First make silhouettes of each child in the class. This can be done by having the student stand between a strong light source and a piece of drawing paper. Quickly trace the shadow with a pencil and then cut it out and mount it on a piece of paper of contrasting color. This may prove to be time-consuming but it gives the teacher a chance to be alone with each individual for a short time.

Every day post one of the silhouettes in the room and tell the class whose it is. At some time during the day, have each child, except the one whose silhouette is featured, write what he or she sees as the best characteristics—the things that they like most— about the featured person.

At the end of the day compile these statements into a paragraph and post the silhouette and the paragraph in the hall for the entire building to see. Make sure they are not placed in a location where they are likely to be defaced. One class has used the silhouettes as gifts to their parents at Christmas and Mother's and Father's Days.

Adopted from Sally Walker,
The University School, Northern Illinois University.

No more fiendish punishment could be desired, were such a thing physically possible, than that one should be turned loose in society and remain absolutely unnoticed by all the members thereof.

William James
The Principles of Psychology

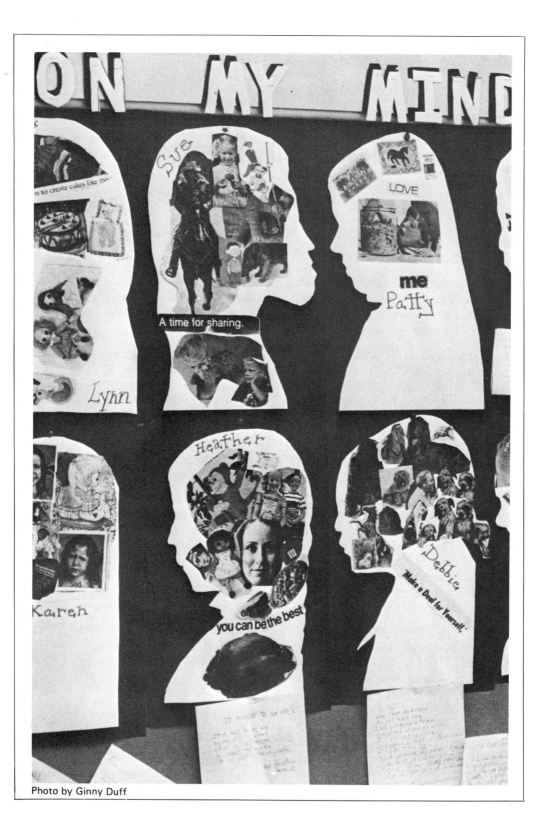

Photo by Ginny Duff

25

on my mind

A variation on Social Silhouettes is called On My Mind.

Ask the students to pair up and draw a large profile or silhouette of one another's heads. Then they are to cut out words, pictures, etc., that represent their personal thoughts, thus making a collage of their current concerns. Later these pictures can be shared with the class.

This activity legitimizes the private thoughts of each student as proper subject matter and as reasonable data to share, as well as allowing the teacher to see what are the primary concerns of his or her students. Another outcome is that students usually begin to realize that they are not alone in many of their concerns. The realization that others share their concerns and feelings often helps students feel "less weird," "less strange," and more "normal," thus enlarging their self-concepts.

Suggested by Carlie Lister,
Wildwood Elementary School, Amherst, Massachusetts

If facts are the seeds that later produce knowledge and wisdom, then the emotions and the impressions of the senses are the fertile soil in which the seeds must grow.

Rachael L. Carson
The Sense of Wonder

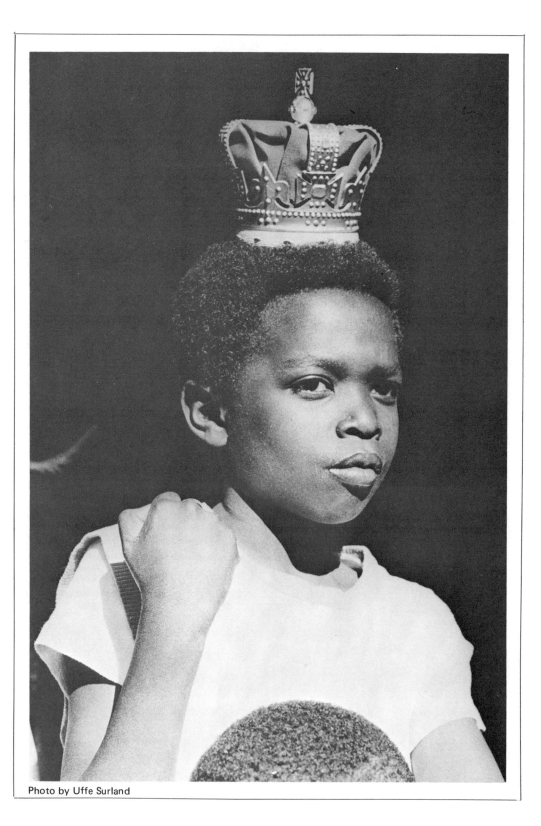

Photo by Uffe Surland

26

meaningful symbols

Divide a blackboard or sheet of newsprint into as many sections as there are students and then ask each student to draw a symbol or picture of something that is meaningful to him—something he is concerned about, that he likes, dislikes, hates, or loves.

One by one, ask each student to explain his drawing and to tell the class why it has meaning for him.

This seemingly simple exercise has a great impact on students. In peer-group situations students seldom have an opportunity to talk about the things that concern them. In addition to discovering that other people share some of the same deep concerns, the student will experience the ideas, feelings, and thoughts of others as being worthwhile and important; he will thus begin to believe in himself as more worthwhile and important also.

This exercise is adapted from the Self-Enhancing Education Project.
(For further information write:
SEE, 1957 Pruneridge Avenue, Santa Clara, California 95050.)

A person learns significantly only those things which he perceives as being involved in the maintenance of, or enhancement of, the structure of self.

Carl R. Rogers

Perceiving, Behaving, and Becoming

27

object sharing

Working in a small group, bring an object to the group and say, "I would like share something with you that gives me a good feeling." Explain why the object is meaningful to you. For example, "Here is a necklace that someone I like very much gave to me. Whenever I wear it, I am reminded of that person and I get a good feeling." Then, "I would like to give you a chance to share something with us and tell us how it gives you a good feeling."

In the "Magic Circle" in the classroom the teacher asks the children to obtain something to bring back to the circle. One by one, they are given an opportunity to share their object with the group. Sometimes this can take place over several days as youngsters bring sentimental objects from home.

This is illustrative of the type of excellent activities included in the Human Development Program by Uvaldo Palomares, Geraldine Ball, and Harold Bessell. (For more information about this program write to: Human Development Training Institute, 7574 University Avenue, La Mesa, California 92041.

The student takes his self-concept with him wherever he goes. . . . Are we influencing that self-concept in positive or negative ways? We need to ask ourselves these kinds of questions. How can a person feel liked unless somebody likes him? How can a person feel wanted unless somebody wants him? How can a person feel accepted unless somebody accepts him? How can a person feel he's a person with dignity and integrity unless somebody treats him so? And how can a person feel that he is capable unless he has some success?

Arthur W. Combs
The Human Side of Learning

28

THE CARD GAME

This activity is the completion of unfinished sentences. On separate poster-board cards are printed such sentence stubs as

If I were older. . .	I wish. . .	Reading. . .
My favorite place. . .	I can't understand why. . .	Other kids. . .
When I make a mistake. . .		

Older students may wish to construct their own unfinished sentences.

The teacher and the students form a circle. Small groups of three to eight seem optimal for the best communication and participation. The game calls for each person to finish a sentence as he wishes. It should be emphasized that there is no right answer, and that the sentence may be funny or serious, true or not true, whatever the speaker chooses. This seems to relieve anxiety for some group members who are not yet ready to be open and honest about their ideas or feelings.

The teacher then asks one child to pick a card, read it to himself, and respond if he wishes by saying the finished sentence aloud. If the student does not feel like saying anything himself, he may hold the card up for the others to see and give them the opportunity to respond. Each child is encouraged to respond to a card as many times as he wishes.

Often in this activity one sentence leads to a lengthy and valuable interchange of ideas and feelings before a card is put away. Children are often curious to hear their peers' feelings and thus the activity may also be used to develop listening skills. Shy children, when not pressured to speak, may feel free to volunteer. Even a silent member can gain confidence when he hears other people of his age expressing feelings that he shares but cannot voice.

Allowing a child to "own" his personal feelings and reactions has a strong impact on his self-esteem. It permits him to say, "It's all right to be me. My inner experiences are legitimate even when they differ from my folks! Having certain feelings at certain times in no way detracts from my value as a person."

Dorothy Corkille Briggs
Your Child's Self-Esteem

29

killer statements and gestures

Conduct a class discussion around the following questions:

Have you ever worked very hard at something you felt was not understood or appreciated? What was it? What was said or done that made you feel your effort was not appreciated?

Have you ever wanted to share things—ideas, feelings, something you've written or made—but were afraid to? Were you afraid that people might put you or it down?" What kinds of things might they say or do that would put you, your ideas, or your achievements down?

Introduce the concept of "killer statements and gestures" to the students. All of us have many feelings, thoughts, and creative behaviors that are killed off by other people's negative comments, physical gestures, etc. Some killer statements that are often used (even by teachers!) are:

> We don't have time for that now.
> That's a stupid idea. You know that's impossible.
> You're really weird!
> Are you crazy? retarded? kidding me? serious?
> Only girls/boys do that!
> Wow, he's strange, man, really strange!
> That stuff's for sissies.

Tell the students that they're going to be social science researchers for the day. Ask them to keep a record of all the killer statements they hear in school, at lunch, at home, and at play. Discuss the findings with them during the next class.

Here is another exercise that can help students identify and legitimize some of their hostile feelings which they may be channeling into killer statements. This activity also helps the students discharge some of these feelings in a way that is not psychologically harmful to the other students.

Ask the students to stand up. When you say "go!" they are to say or shout all the killer statements that they have heard in during the class. Tell them to use all the killer statements, gestures, and sounds they want to. They can shout at the air, their desk, chair, or whatever else feels comfortable.

Some other ideas are to have students make collages of killer statements and gestures. They can discuss how killer statements serve them. Questions can be asked such as: "What do killer statements protect you from?" Are there things that you would really like to say but are afraid to disclose and therefore you substitute killer statements?— for instance, saying "That's for sissies!' instead of 'I'd like to do that, but I probably wouldn't do it very well' or 'That's not a bad shot for a girl' instead of 'I, like you.' V'

The most deadly of all sins is the mutilation of a child's spirit.

Erik H. Erikson
Young Man Luther

30

positive mantram

No matter what you say or do to me, I'm still a worthwhile person!

Ask the students to close their eyes and repeat in unison with you the chant:
"No matter what you say or do to me, I'm still a worthwhile person!"
This seemingly simple exercise has a very powerful impact if done repeatedly.
It implants a new seed thought in each of the students; it acts as an antidote to
all the negative thoughts and statements already implanted in their thinking.

A way to heighten the effect of this exercise is to ask students to imagine the face of
someone who has put them down in some way in the past—a parent, teacher, coach,
friend, fellow student, Girl Scout leader, policeman, etc.—each time they begin to say
"No matter. . ." Have them stick out their chins and repeat the sentence strongly
and convincingly.

After they get the hang of it you might interject statements like "You're stupid, ugly,
etc.," and let them respond to these with "No matter what you say or do to me, I'm
still a worthwhile person."

We learned this exercise from Leonard Smith.

*Take, for example, the 2nd grade teacher who has as one of her missions the
encouragement, if not establishment, of subject-verb agreement in the language
of her pupils. The goal is clear and its approximation is measurable and a fair
segment of the community thinks it a defensible goal.*

*And consider this teacher who asked her children to draw a picture about how
they felt and to write underneath the picture some words to explain it.
And consider the child, carrying out this assignment, who drew a picture of
a tombstone with his initials on it and under that wrote, "sometimes I
wish I was dead." And consider this teacher whose response was to cross out*
was *and to write in* were. *That teacher's clarity (and singularity) of purpose
is precisely what kept her from being the teacher she could have been in
that setting with that child at that moment.*

Media and Methods,
March 1970, p. 43.

31

dear me letter

It is important for the student to be able to integrate and find meaning in his experiences. A "Dear Me" letter at the end of an exercise or a class can serve this purpose. It can also serve as an effective means of ongoing evaluation for the teacher.

Ask each student to individually take time to integrate his experience by writing a letter to himself. You can suggest questions or statements to facilitate the writing, such as:

> What was the high point of the session?
> What was the low point?
> I learned that I. . .
> I felt. . .
> I relearned. . .
> What was unique about your response?
> What was typical of your behavior?
> How honest were you when you were sharing?
> What about your behavior did you like the most?
> What about your behavior did you like the least?
> I need. . .
> I am concerned about. . .
> I wonder. . .
> This class would have been better if only. . .
> If only I. . .
> I appreciated myself for. . .

These letters can be written in the journals, or they can be handed in to the teacher. To do both, have the students use a piece of carbon paper. The original stays in the journal; the carbon is handed in to you. Students who wish to keep some of their responses private might remove the carbon paper while recording these responses.

Contributed by Joel Goodman
University of Massachusetts

Self-expression leads to growth and expanded awareness. Those who stifle themselves for fear of criticism "pay the piper in dis-ease and the stunted growth of personality and psyche. Those who express themselves unfold in health, beauty and human potential. They become unblocked channels through which creativity, intuition and inspiration can flow.

Christopher Hills and Robert B. Stone
Conduct Your Own Awareness Session

32

re-entry questions

During the first few weeks of working in small groups, it is a good idea to open each session with a re-entry question. These questions are designed to re-establish the level of group rapport that has been developed, as well as to positively enhance the self-concepts of the participants.

Some of the following suggestions have been described in earlier portions of this book. You may find them fun to do again or simply skip over them, perhaps saving them for a later date. Here are some useful re-entry questions.

What is the most exciting thing that has happened to you in the last week? Over the weekend? Yesterday? What is the most exciting thing you did?

Suppose you have a magic box; it can be any size or shape. In it can be anything you want that would make you happy. What is in your box that makes you extremely happy?

Suppose a doctor had just told you that you have only one year left to live. What would you do differently? How would you change your life? (This exercise can be used in conjunction with goal-setting. For example, "What is stopping you from doing some of these things now? Let's set a goal to achieve some of those things.") Suppose you only had one hour to live, starting right now—what would you do?

Share with the group an experience in which you made someone happy. In which someone made you happy.

If you could teach everybody in the world just one thing—an idea, a skill, a precept, a fact—what would it be?

What would you say has been the greatest learning experience of your life? Of the past week?

If you could be talented in something you are not talented in now, what would it be? Why? Is it something that would please you? please others?

If you could be any person in the world, who would you be? Why?

If you could live anywhere in the world, where would it be? Why?

In the light of the influence of the self-concept on academic achievement, it would seem like a good idea for schools to follow the precept I saw printed on an automobile drag-strip racing program: "Every effort is made to ensure that each entry has a reasonable chance of victory."

William W. Purkey
Self-Concept and School Achievement

33

REFLECTIVE LISTENING

Give all participants a sheet of drawing paper that is cut to be a piece of a larger puzzle. Indicate the "up" side of the paper and put a big background for the puzzle with the shapes drawn on it on the floor in the middle of the circle (see illustration). You can use the background over and over. Tell the participants to draw a symbol of our times, a symbol of what is happening in the world right now. Tell them to make it their own symbol, a symbol of their feelings about our era or times. When they are done tell them to put their piece on the puzzle background.

Now you should say something like: "The name of this exercise is Reflective Listening. Very often we seem to listen to the words others say, when the more important message may be the *feelings* expressed behind the words. Our purpose here is to give ourselves practice in hearing another person's feelings and in checking out whether or not we are hearing correctly. Another result of this practice will be the experience of having *your* feelings heard. I'll try to show you what I mean—is there any symbol you would particularly like to hear about?" A participant then tells about his symbol (usually there is little reluctance). Then you, as leader, attempt to reflect the participant's feelings: "You feel hopeless." "no, not exactly." "Powerless to do anything?" "Yeah, powerless and lonely too, sometimes."

It is important to make the distinction between feelings *in the symbol* and feelings *in the person.* The frequency with which people invest the picture rather than the person with feelings points up the need for this activity. We prefer that each person whose symbol is described and whose feelings the group attempts to reflect responds affirmatively to one of these questions before the group goes on: "Do you think your feelings of this particular moment have been heard?" "Would you like to stop now even though your feelings may not have been completely heard?"

One of the most important aspects of this lesson is the developing awareness of the language of feelings. This language can be developed inductively as the class proceeds, or can be introduced by the leader. At the beginning of the second session with the symbols (it is usually impossible to complete this exercise in less th an three sessions) we have introduced the notion that feeling can be thought of as having a direction: pleasure/love characterizing one direction; and pain/hate the other. Word lists for feelings in each of these directions can be listed under their general headings on butcher paper hung on the wall. This procedure can facilitate broader participation in the reflecting process.

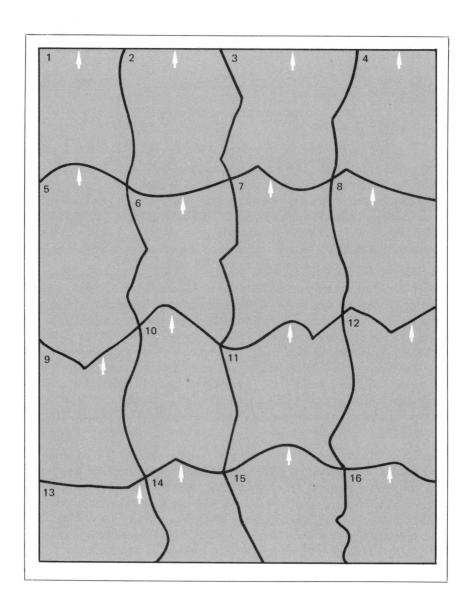

Experience has shown this to be an activity with considerable transfer to students' daily life. Students frequently attest to listening for the feelings in the statements of their parents, teachers, classmates, and others after doing this exercise.

We learned this exercise from
Elizabeth Achterman, Self-Enhancing Education Project.

"First of all," he said, *"if you can learn a simple trick, Scout, you'll get along a lot better with all kinds of folks. You never really understand a person until you consider things from his point of view. . ."*
"Sir?"
". . .until you climb into his skin and walk around in it."

Harper Lee
To Kill a Mockingbird

34

teacher feedback

It is important that the students in your classes feel that they can give you honest feedback about the way they experience your behavior toward them. It is also useful for you to know how your actions are perceived by your students. The following techniques can be used to elicit feedback from your students.

Metaphor Game: What are you feeling right now about me? If you could imagine me as an animal, what animal would you choose? Please try to describe me as an animal in terms of how you perceive me. Then tell us why I remind you of the animal you choose. For example, "I see you as my cat, Blue. You seem calm like my cat."

Anonymous Writing: Have the children write what they like and dislike about you, the classroom environment, their studies, the rules, etc.

Strength Training: Sometime when you have a few extra minutes, try eliciting feedback in the following manner. Write the following on the chalkboard: Mr./Mrs. (your name) is _____ . I feel _____ when he/she (does what). Have the students first write their answers down. Then ask them to read their answers while you record them on the chalkboard. Ask for clarification when you don't understand what the student has written. Ask for a specific example of your behavior. When this is completed, if there are things that you wish to change in your behavior, you might ask the class or a group of fellow teachers to brainstorm alternative ways of behaving to produce the sought-after effect.

Letters: Have a letter box in your class where children can correspond in writing with you. Answer all the letters that are signed.

Report Card: At the end of a grading period, distribute to each student a facsimile report card. Then instruct the students to grade *you,* commenting on your attitude and effort toward the class for future suggestions on what could be changed or further developed to improve the learning situation. Follow-through involves trying some of these suggestions.

These activities take great courage on your part. In the kind of collaborative teaching-learning environment we feel should be encouraged, these activities mean a great deal both to you and to the students. It seems likely that a student sincerely asked to help his teacher would feel better about himself as a result of his teacher's trust.

> *The degree to which I can create relationships which facilitate the growth of others as separate persons is a measure of the growth I have achieved in myself.*
>
> Carl R. Rogers
> *Perceiving, Behaving, and Becoming*

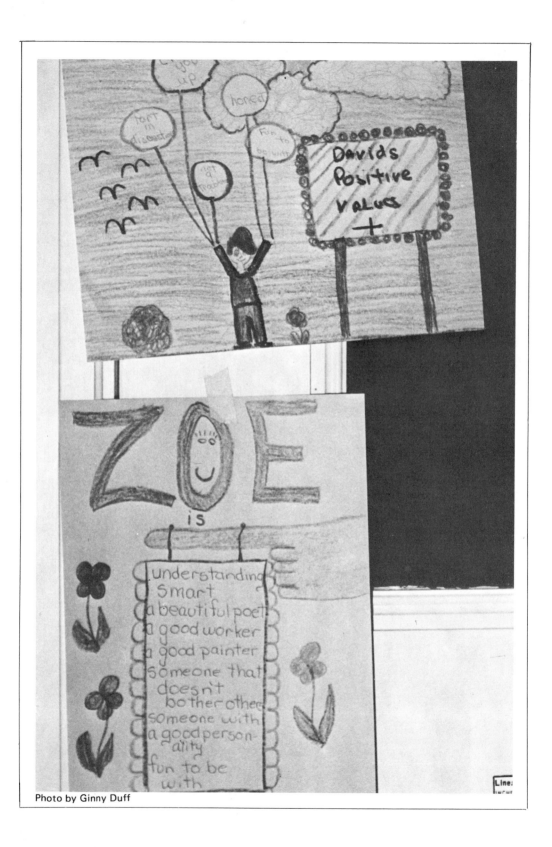

Photo by Ginny Duff

35

operation self-image

The Hugoton, Kansas, Public Schools have a Title III ESEA project entitled "Operation Self-Image," directed by Clark J. Milson, Ed.D. In a recent newsletter Glen Kirkendall, a third-grade teacher, shared some of the activities he uses. We pass them on to you:

I believe the *physical environment* in a classroom can influence the way a child feels about himself and others, as well as his attitude toward school in general. For these reasons I pay much attention to things like bulletin boards, charts, and other stimuli which students observe each day. The following activities have been tried and proven effective in my classroom:

The entrance door to the room displays a large sign with the words: "Today is _____ _____ Day!" Each child in the room puts his name on the sign in turn and is allowed to do all the classroom chores that day. In addition, classmates are encouraged to do all they can to make the chosen child's day a good one.

Smiling faces cut out from tagboard and colored with various colors are hung from the ceiling on pieces of yarn. This gives a subtle feeling of happiness even when a child is looking at the ceiling. Other materials of this sort are placed around the room in locations where children will see them during the course of the day.

A large but inexpensive full-length mirror is hanging by the door so students may get better acquainted with their physical appearance.

Old Timex watch display cases may be obtained from stores which sell this product. The cases make excellent places for children to display articles of interest and hobby material. This permits a child to *share* a bit of his "Secret Self" or the things about himself that he might not otherwise disclose.

Keeping pets is another aspect of education I like to advance. Tropical fish, hamsters, guinea pigs, and sea horses have been residents in our room this year—not to mention the tarantula and the 13-lined ground squirrel. Caring for pets helps a child to develop a *sense of responsibility* and a feeling of importance.

The Self-Image Program provides stationery for teachers to write "Greatness Notes" to students. When a child does something outstanding, he may receive a note congratulating him for his achievement. This activity makes both parents and students feel successful.

The bulletin board I like most is entitled, "Getting to Know _____." I start the year with my name and a set of pictures of me doing things I like to do but things which children seldom see me doing at school. Each picture is keyed to an explanation which I write on a separate piece of paper and staple to the board with the pictures. Each child has his or her time on the board before school is out. They enjoy having their own pictures up, and also enjoy the pictures classmates bring.

36
positive reinforcement: an instructional solution

My first experience with positive reinforcement as a prevailing instructional technique occurred when I started my U.S. History course by giving everybody an"A." Or, to be more accurate, I gave everybody 600 points. Each week the students took a 40-point quiz. Exams were also given a predetermined number of points. Each quiz and exam was returned with the total number of points remaining to the student after I graded it. When their total dropped below 540, they had a "B." Below 500 they had a "C," etc. A funny thing happened that year. Nobody failed the course, with one exception by virtue of absences. Two sophomore students received the first "A" in their lives. Since they had seldom even earned a "B" in the previous thirteen years, I asked them how they were able to get an "A" all of a sudden. Their reply: this was the first time anybody had ever held out the hope of their getting an "A." They assumed it would be the last time, too. So they studied hard to keep it. I wonder what kind of students they would have been if their previous education had provided hope?

I adopted another simple technique of positive reinforcement: I gave away my red pencils. Think about it a moment: red symbolizes violence, blood, STOP, (immoral, godless) communism—a whole host of authoritarian, painful, paranoiac associations. On a student's paper it essentially means: "Here, stupid, is where you were stupid!" Red is negative reinforcement all the way. Editors have a reputation for being merciless, but even *they* use *blue* pencils.

The best system of positive reinforcement is, of course, to evaluate a student's work from the viewpoint of what is right with it rather than from that of what is wrong with it. Show the student what he has going for him. Point out his strengths. Show him how he can develop his strengths; that is, treat error in the context of nurturing capacity rather than as a process of revealing ignorance. The student already knows he's ignorant. That's the one thing they succeeded in teaching him before he got to you. Now he needs to know that he can do something about his ignorance.

The best way to affirm student performance via grading is to give grades only for that which can be affirmed. A number of junior colleges have adopted a grading system wherein no record is established in a course until the student has met the requirements for a passing grade. He can still fail a course (or courses), and thus suffer the attendant loss of money, time, and effort, plus all the discouragement and disappointment that goes with it. That is, he still suffers the *consequences* of failure, but no punishment.

Negative grades are, after all, primarily punitive. Sort of like fining a fellow $500 for being broke.

by Noel McInnis, Director,
Center for Curriculum Design, Evanston, Illinois.
Reprinted from *Association for Humanistic Psychology Newsletter*.

37
quickies

1. *Do Well:* Sitting in a circle, ask the children to share with the group something they like to do and that they do well.
2. *Pen Pal:* Ask the students to write a letter describing themselves to an imaginary pen pal. Encourage them to go beyond mere physical descriptions, adding things like hobbies, family composition, favorite subjects, etc.
3. *My Body:* Ask the students to consider the following: What are the beautiful parts of your body? The ugliest? Where did you get your notions of beauty? How do TV commercials effect your notion of beauty? How does your body influence yourself? What are bodies for, anyway?
4. *My Assets:* Ask students to write a paragraph about themselves describing the assets they have, the negative traits they would like to eliminate, and the positive characteristics they would like to obtain or develop. In dealing with the negative aspects, it is important to distinguish between things that can be changed (a bad disposition) and things that cannot be changed (a weak chin).
5. *Puppets:* Ask a group of elementary students to work alone or together to make up a story about themselves. Then have them make hand puppets representing the characters and to act out the story they have written. Encourage them to focus on the positive qualities of the participants.
6. *Self-Worth:* Have the students write a story about something they can do to make other people feel worthy.
7. *Drawing:* Ask the students to draw a picture of the things they do that make them feel good about themselves.
8. *Get Well:* When a student is sick for an extended period of time, initiate a class project to make or buy a gift for the sick child. One class we know of constructed a giant "We miss you!" card from individual paintings done by the children. The effect of caring and giving is as powerful on the class as is the effect of receiving and being cared for on the child who is ill.
9. *Class Mural:* Tape a long sheet of butcher paper to the wall, provide the class with lots of crayons, and ask the students to draw a "class mural" depicting the things they do in common and the things they do that are more uniquely their own.
10. *"Proud-Of" Bulletin Boards:* Create a large bulletin board in your room just for posting individual and group work, kids' pictures and drawings. The bulletin board should always be plastered with pictures and the work of the kids. Some

ideas teachers have used successfully are "What Would You Like To Be?"
(pictures of occupational choice with stories written by children displayed by
the picture that matches their choice). "I Am Proud Of" (Stories and pictures
drawn by students illustrating an achievement or an event they are proud of).
Polaroid pictures of kids next to correct homework, poems, stories, and
drawings they have created are also very reinforcing. Names and pictures should
change weekly in order to give everyone recognition for something every two or
three weeks. Use your ingenuity to discover strengths in each student. (This was
suggested by James Hawkins, Bethune Elementary School, Pontiac, Michigan.)

11. *Classroom or School Newspaper:* The creation of a classroom newspaper is a
    good way to provide children with the opportunity to see their names and their
    work in print. Articles can also be written about the children's achievements.
    Recognition, in print, of positive services, activities, and achievements does a
    lot to increase and improve self-concept. Students can select the name of the
    paper, choose editors and reporters, conduct interviews, and draw illustrations.

    On a school basis, each room could have a reporter, who might change from
    time to time, to collect and gather material for publication. The writing of the
    newspaper also helps strengthen written language skills. The newspaper could
    also be used in various classrooms for reading instruction.

12. *Write a Story:* Ask the students to write a story about themselves as "neat"
    people. Specifically instruct them to deal with personality and character—what
    they like about the way they are. In other words, discourage them from thinking
    of themselves as only their talents, skills, or achievements, but rather their
    feelings, thoughts, and behaviors.

13. *The Nicest Thing Ever:* Have the whole class write *The Nicest Thing Ever* book.
    Let each child write and illustrate two contributions:
    (a) The Nicest Thing I Ever Did for Anyone" (ask them to explain what it was,
        why they did it, and how it made them feel).
    (b) "The Nicest Thing Anyone Ever Did for Me" (ask them to describe it, why
        they think someone did it, and how it made a difference in what might have
        happened).
    (c) "The Nicest Thing I Ever Did for Myself."

14. *Teaching:* Ask students to share with the class one area in which they feel
    confident enough to teach another person. This could be a hobby, a skill, a
    sport, a musical instrument, a special interest, etc. Also, ask them what they
    would like to learn if someone in the class had the skill to teach them.

15. *Inheritance Fantasy:* Tell the students to imagine a rich uncle has just died,
    leaving them $10,000 in his will with the stipulation that they must give it away.
    "What would they do with the money?"

16. *Breaking a Record:* Ask students what record they would break if they could
    break any record in the world. Why would they do it?

17. *It's Neat to be Me!:* Ask the students to consider the fact that they are one of a
    kind. Encourage them to write a short poem (or story) entitled "It's Neat to be
    Me!" This should be a free exercise, not a forced writing assignment.

18. *I Can:* Ask the students to write a story about a boy or girl who faces a physical
    test of courage and resourcefulness and succeeds; or a story about a teenager
    who suddenly finds himself in trouble and gets out of it.

19. *Flower:* Have students discuss or write their responses to the following questions:
    If they were a flower, what kind would they be? What color? Where would they be

planted? If they were picked, who would pick them? To whom would they like to be given? Where would they like to be placed? (Idea from Tom Quinlan)

20. *Graffiti Board:* Get some butcher paper or newsprint and designate an area where kids can write or draw anything they want. It's their place to let off steam in a nondestructive way. Periodically place new paper over the old so that new graffiti can be collected.

The test of a society, as of an institution, is not whether it is improving, although certainly such a test is relevant, but whether it is adequate to the needs of the present and of the forseeable future. Our educating institutions fail that test: schools, colleges, churches, newspapers, magazines, television stations and networks, all fall short of what they could be, of what they must *be if we are to find meaning and purpose in our lives, in our society, and in our world.*

Charles E. Silberman
Crisis in the Classroom

two
my strengths

We've maintained (along with others, notably Herbert Otto and Jack Gibb) that the most effective way to enhance a person's capacity to develop his full potential is to concentrate on his strengths. Negativism and "attacking" type procedures seem to us to be inappropriate, and especially so in the school setting.

You'll find the activities in this section interesting. It is unfortunate but true that many youngsters feel that they have no strengths—just as you have probably found that they had a hard time acknowledging pride and successful occasions in the previous section. To some extent this is a manifestation of our cultural emphasis on humility. In our society it is not usually deemed "proper" to indicate pride or pleasure at one's successes and strengths. That's too bad, we feel. We'd like to see people secure in the knowledge that they can do many things well. In fact, a "you can do it" attitude is one we wish teachers would continuously foster. Obviously, some people cover up a deep sense of "I'm *not* OK" by blustering, bragging behavior. These people, too, need a firmer conviction of their real strengths so they don't have to constantly "ego trip."

Herbert Otto and John Mann summarized the intent of this section very well when they wrote:

> One of the findings of the Human Potentialities Research Project has been that the average, healthy, well-functioning person has a very limited awareness of his personality strengths and resources but has a much clearer idea of his weaknesses and problem areas. On the other hand, it has been found that the process of taking inventory of one's strengths and personality assets is experienced as strengthening, brings gains in self-confidence and improves the self-image.[1]

---

[1] Herbert Otto and John Mann, "Human Potential," in Herbert Otto (ed.), *Human Potentialities* (St. Louis: Warren H. Green, Inc., 1968) p. 143.

THE ANIMAL SCHOOL:

The Administration of the School Curriculum
with References to Individual Differences

Dr. George H. Reavis
Assistant Superintendent, Cincinnati Public Schools, 1939-1948

Once upon a time, the animals decided they must do something heroic to meet the problems of "a new world." So they organized a school.

They adopted an activity curriculum consisting of running, climbing, swimming, and flying. To make it easier to administer the curriculum *all* the animals took *all* the subjects.

The duck was excellent in swimming, in fact better than his instructor; but he made only passing grades in flying and was very poor in running. Since he was slow in running, he had to stay after school and also drop swimming in order to practice running. This was kept up until his web feet were badly worn and he was only average in swimming. *But average was acceptable in school so nobody worried about that except the duck.*

The rabbit started at the top of the class in running, but had a nervous breakdown because of so much make-up work in swimming.

The squirrel was excellent in climbing until he developed frustration in the flying class where his teacher made him start from the ground up instead of from the tree top down. He also developed a "charlie horse" from over-exertion and then got C in climbing and D in running.

The eagle was a problem child and was disciplined severely. In the climbing class he beat all the others to the top of the tree, but insisted on using his own way to get there.

At the end of the year, an abnormal eel that could swim exceedingly well, and also run, climb, and fly a little, had the highest average and was valedictorian.

The prairie dogs stayed out of school and fought the tax levy because the administration would not add digging and burrowing to the curriculum. They apprenticed their children to a badger and later joined the groundhogs and gophers to start a successful private school.

Does this fable have a moral?

38
IALAC

The IALAC Story is told to illustrate how one's self-concept can be destroyed by others. If done with feeling and imagination, it can be a very powerful and moving experience. We have found that it is appropriate for students of all ages.

Take a sheet of paper and write the letters IALAC (pronounced I-ah-lack) on it in large bold print. Holding this to your chest so that the students can see it, tell them, "Everyone carries an invisible IALAC sign around with them at all times and wherever they go. IALAC stands for 'I am lovable and capable.' This is our self-concept, or how we feel about ourselves. The size of our sign—or how good we feel about ourselves—is often affected by how others interact with us. If somebody is nasty to us, teases us, puts us down, rejects us, hits us, etc., then a piece of our IALAC sign is destroyed. [Illustrate this by tearing a corner piece off the sign.] I am going to tell you a story to illustrate how this happens in everyday life." Then proceed to tell the students about a boy or girl who is the same age they are. Pick a name that no one in the class has. As you tell the story, try to be as emotional and dramatic as you can without burlesquing it too much. An outline is provided below. You will have to fill it in with your own imagination. Some teachers we know have the children help create the story as they go along. As you describe each event that negatively affects the student's IALAC sign, tear another piece of the sign off until at the end you are left with almost nothing.

A possible outline for the IALAC story is as follows. Feel free to adapt, add to, change, and embellish it in any way you want:

> A seventh-grade boy named Michael is still lying in bed three minutes after his alarm goes off. All of a sudden his mother calls to him, "Michael, you lazy-head, get your body out of bed and get down here before I send your father up there!" (rip!) Michael gets out of bed, goes to get dressed, and can't find a clean pair of socks. His mother tells him he'll have to wear yesterday's pair. (rip!) He goes to brush his teeth and his older sister, who's already locked herself in the bathroom, tells him to drop dead! (rip!) He goes to breakfast to find soggy cereal waiting for him. (rip!) As he leaves for school, he forgets his lunch and his mother calls to him, "Michael you've forgotten your lunch; you'd forget your head if it weren't attached!" (rip!) As he gets to the corner he sees the school bus pull away and so he has to walk to school. (rip!) He's late to school and has to get a pass from the principal who gives him a lecture. (rip!)

Photo by Ginny Duff

Continue the story through the school day with appropriate examples. Some possibilities are:

> Forgetting his homework
> Getting a 68 on a spelling test
> Being called on for the only homework question he can't answer
> Making a mistake in reading so that all the kids laugh
> Being picked last to play ball at recess
> Dropping his tray in the lunchroom, with everybody applauding
> Being picked on by bullies on the way home from school
> Being referred to as "Hey you!" in gym class

You can think of other examples or get the students to help you.

When Michael gets home from school some typical negative events might include not being able to watch the baseball game because his mother is watching her favorite soap opera or because he has not yet finished his homework, or being told to wash the dishes for the third night in a row because his older brother has band practice, etc.

End the story by showing Michael going to bed with an IALAC sign about as big as a quarter! When you finish, ask the kids to discuss the following questions:

> How does *your* IALAC sign get torn up? What things affect you the most?
> What do you do that destroys the IALAC signs of others—in school, family, etc.?
> How do you feel when your IALAC sign is ripped? When you rip someone else's?
> What can we do to help people enlarge their signs rather than make them smaller?

This exercise can also be used in conjunction with Exercise 29—Killer Statements and Gestures. In the exercises that follow, activities are presented that help students paste their own and others' IALAC signs back together again. Exercise 30—"Positive Mantram"—can also be used in relation to IALAC, with the idea that whenever someone tries to rip your IALAC sign, you can simply repeat the mantram: "No matter what you say or do to me, I'm still a worthwhile person."

One class we know of spent a whole week wearing IALAC signs and actually ripping them apart anytime someone said or did something damaging to their self-concept. Whenever a sign was ripped, the class had to stop and discuss what had just happened. The learning that took place was incredible. Several teachers have enthusiastically reported trying this with their families. Have fun with it. It is a powerful technique.

The IALAC story was originally conceived by Sidney Simon and Merrill Harmin. Simon has recently written and published the story for use by students and teachers. For a copy, write Argus Communications, 7440 Natchez Avenue, Niles, Illinois 60648.

> *Love and self-worth are so intertwined that they may properly be related through the use of the term* identity. *Thus we may say that the single basic need that people have is the requirement for an identity; the belief that we are someone in distinction to others, and that the someone is important and worthwhile. Then* love *and* self-worth *may be considered the two pathways that mankind has discovered that lead to a successful identity.*
>
> William Glasser, M.D.
> *Schools Without Failure*

39

personal evaluation sheet

The personal evaluation sheet is an informal, nonthreatening worksheet designed to help students clarify and verbalize their feelings about themselves in relation to everyday experiences. The evaluation sheet can be readily adapted to meet the requirements of a wide range of grade levels by alterations of the substance and structure of the questions.

The dittoed evaluation sheets are composed of sentence stubs or questions intended to stimulate responses about the concerns and attitudes shared by all children. Although the process itself is the primary objective of this activity, the feedback is often useful for future planning and follow-up.

Listed below are some suggested sentence stubs and questions that can be used on evaluation sheets. It is recommended that the number of questions be limited to ten or twelve. Questions may be deleted, added, or modified to fit classroom needs.

Today I feel very. . .	I enjoy reading about. . .
I enjoy. . .	I wish grownups would (wouldn't). . .
I am unhappy when. . .	I like myself best when. . .
I feel good when. . .	If I had a choice, I would. . .
I wish my teacher(s). . .	At school I am. . .
My classmates think I. . .	I wish. . .
School is. . .	Tomorrow I would like to. . .

With younger children it is sometimes useful to use questions that can be answered with "yes," "no," or "sometimes."

Do you like school? Your teacher? Your classmates?
Do you like yourself?
Are you a quiet person? A noisy person?
Are you an active person?
Are you usually happy? Unhappy?
Do you have many friends? A best friend?

Do you have fun at school? At home? Outside?
Did you like answering these questions?

From the *Handbook for the Human Relations Approach to Teaching,*
Human Relations Education Center of the Buffalo Public Schools,
James J. Foley, Director

There is no value judgment more important to man—no factor more decisive in his psychological development and motivation—than the estimate he passes on himself.

Nathaniel Branden
The Psychology of Self-Esteem

40
strength bombardment

Have the students break into groups of five or six, preferably with other students they know well and feel comfortable with. Focusing on one person at a time, the group is to bombard him with all the strengths they see in him. The person being bombarded should remain silent until the group has finished. One member of the group should act as recorder, listing the strengths and giving them to the person when the group has finished.

The students should be instructed to list at least fifteen strengths for each student. They should also be cautioned that no "put-down" statements are allowed. Only positive assets are to be mentioned. At the end of the exercise ask the students to discuss how they felt giving and receiving positive feedback. Was one easier than the other? Which one?

In some groups it is wise to spend ten minutes discussing with the class the different types of strengths that exist, as well as developing a vocabulary of strength words they can use. It may be a good thing to list all the words that are "brainstormed" on the chalkboard for the students to look at during the "bombardment" sessions.

To reinforce this activity, have your students also ask their parents to list the strengths they see in them. The new list could be added to that which is collected in class. This additional exercise will also provide the student with some very important positive feedback from his parents.

Note to teachers: Haim Ginott in his book *Teacher and Child* (New York: Macmillan, 1972) makes the following useful distinction between evaluative feedback and appreciative feedback: evaluative feedback is characterized by judgment—i.e., the teacher is the judge and the student is to be judged. Examples of this kind of feedback are: "*This* is a B— poem." "*You* are a good artist." "*You* are funny."

Appreciative feedback is characterized by letting the student know how you, as a person, have been affected by what they have done. Examples of appreciative feedback are: "*I* was deeply moved by your poem, *The Me I Never Dared To Be.*" As *I* read it I identified with the many fears you wrote about. *I* guess we are similar in more ways than *I* had imagined." "*I* enjoyed your pictures. *I* like the way you use colors to express motion and power." "*I* appreciate the way you are always able to relax the tension in the classroom with a joke or a story. *I* enjoy your humor."

Try as much as possible to use appreciative feedback with the students in both formal (papers, artwork, etc.) and informal (personal feedback, group discussions, etc.) situations. Try discussing this distinction with your students and encourage them to also use appreciative rather than evaluative feedback with each other. The key to the difference is that most evaluative feedback starts with the word "you"; most appreciative feedback starts with the word "I."

We learned this activity from Herbert Otto.
We recommended his book, *Group Methods Designed to Actualize Human Potential*, available from The Holistic Press, 329 El Camino Drive, Beverly Hills, California 90212.

Everything has its beauty but not everyone sees it.

Confucius

THREE POSSIBLE REASONS

Idries Shah

The Magic Monastery

A dervish was sitting by the roadside when a haughty courtier with his retinue, riding past in the opposite direction, struck him with a cane, shouting:

"Out of the way, you miserable wretch!"

When they had swept past, the dervish rose and called after them:

"May you attain all that you desire in the world, even up to its highest ranks!"

A bystander, much impressed by this scene, approached the devout man and said to him:

"Please tell me whether your words were motivated by generosity of spirit, or because the desires of the world will undoubtedly corrupt that man even more?"

"O man of bright countenance," said the dervish, "has it not occurred to you that I said what I did because people who attain their real desires would not need to ride about striking dervishes?"

41
the nourishing game

The following exercise is a variation of the previous one, Strength Bombardment. It is also useful in developing a supportive atmosphere for self-disclosure as well as strengthening the self-concepts of the students.

Working in a small group or with the whole class, ask the students to sit in a circle. Ask each child to think of one or two children in the class who have made him feel good, how this was done, and specifically how he felt good.

Allow each child a turn to share his feelings with as many other children as he cares to. Try to have each student talk directly to the person that made him feel good rather than talking *about* that person. You might also watch for students who don't seem to be receiving any feedback and make a point of telling them how they nourished you.

Suggested by Kathy Phillips

> *Man wishes to be confirmed in his being by man, and wishes to have a presence in the being of the other . . . secretly and bashfully he watches for a Yes which allows him to be and which can come only from one human person to another.*
>
> Martin Buber
> *The Knowledge of Man*

42

student of the week

Place the names of all your students in a box. Each week, in front of the class, draw one of the names from the box. The student whose name is drawn becomes the Student of the Week.

Ask the rest of the class to state the things they like about the chosen student. Be patient and encouraging; stress that everyone has many good qualities. You might also wish to tell the students that it is important to take this seriously because they too will one day have a turn. Try to get six to ten concrete statements listed. It is also a good idea to try to keep the lists equal in length.

Have the Student of the Week bring in a picture of himself, or take one of him with a Polaroid camera. Post his or her picture, name, and list of good qualities on the bulletin board. You may change this bulletin board each week, or you may wish to make a cumulative bulletin board of Students of the Week.

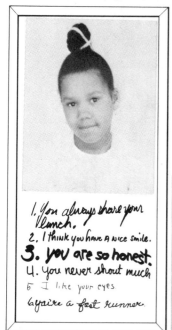

1. You always share your lunch.
2. I think you have a nice smile.
3. You are so honest.
4. You never shout much
5 I like your eyes
6 you're a fast runner.

To assure that all class members receive recognition within a shorter period of time, you may wish to have three students a week (Monday, Wednesday, Friday) or three on one day of the week.

Suggested by Astrid Collins
Markham Junior High School
San Jose, California

You see, really and truly, apart from the things anyone can pick up (the dressing and the proper way of speaking, and so on), the difference between a lady and a flower girl is not how she behaves, but how she's treated. I shall always be a flower girl to Professor Higgins, because he always treats me as a flower girl, and always will; but I know I can be a lady to you, because you always treat me as a lady, and always will.

Eliza Doolittle to Colonel Pickering
in George Bernard Shaw's *Pygmalion*

WHAT IS REAL?

Margery Williams
The Velveteen Rabbit

"What is REAL?" asked the Rabbit one day when they were lying side by side near the nursery fender before Nana came to tidy the room. "Does it mean having things that buzz inside you and a stickout handle?"

"REAL isn't how you are made," said the Skin Horse. "It's a thing that happens to you. When a child loves you for a long, long time, then you become REAL."

"Does it hurt?" asked the Rabbit.

"Sometimes," said the Skin Horse, for he was always truthful. "When you are REAL you don't mind being hurt."

"Does it happen all at once, like being wound up," he asked, "or bit by bit?"

"It doesn't happen all at once," said the Skin Horse. "You become. It takes a long time. That's why it doesn't often happen to people who break easily, or have sharp edges, or have to be carefully kept. Generally, by the time you are REAL, most of your hair has been loved off, and your eyes drop off, and you get loose in the joints and very shabby. But these things don't matter at all because once you are REAL you can't be ugly, except to people who don't understand."

43
MAKING IT REAL

This exercise is designed to help students expand their capacity for self-disclosure and taking risks, expand their repertoire of behavior with others, build up positive feelings about themselves, integrate their internal dichotomies, and reinforce their strengths.

Ask each student to choose what he feels to be one of his greatest strengths as a person. After each has had time to consider this, ask him to find the one word that best described it (i.e., creative, friendly, warm, athletic, intelligent, persevering, etc.). Then ask the students to get up and move around the class like the words they have chosen—to make the whole body *be* this word. In order to dissipate the fear of looking foolish, it is a good idea for the teacher (you) to model this for the class by demonstrating with one of your strengths first.

When everyone is moving, ask the class members to exaggerate their positions as much as possible. When they have done this, ask them to stop where they are and find the opposite of this word (i.e., creative—dull, friendly—hostile, warm—cold, athletic—awkward) and walk around the room in the manner of that word.

Ask them to become the original word again. Then stop and have the class share their feelings about what they have experienced. Try this with several different strengths and compare the outcomes.

If you are working with a particularly inhibited class, you might have the students assume the position that best represents their words, rather than moving in the manner of the words. Later have them switch their positions to represent the opposite of their words. The changing of positions should be done as slowly as possible so the students can experience the changes that occur in their bodies as they move. This exercise can be done with everybody's eyes closed to reduce the stage fright of being observed.

We developed this from an exercise by Janet Lederman.
We highly recommend her book *Anger and the Rocking Chair*
(New York: McGraw-Hill, 1969; paperback, New York: Viking Press, 1973).

> *The great law of culture is to let each one become all that he was created capable of being; expand, if possible, to his full growth; and show himself at length in his own shape and stature, be these what they may.*
>
> Thomas Carlyle

44
nicknames

Almost all children have nicknames. Some are complimentary; many are not! As part of our general orientation, we tend to discover each other's weaknesses, and in words like, Baldy, Fatso, Skinny, Rat, Sissy, Bull, Four-eyes, Dumbo, Ears, Slim, Worm, Stinky, and so on, exploit them.

Although these nicknames are often accepted by children, their effect on a developing self-concept is damaging. To reverse this trend have students give themselves and/or each other nicknames based on their strengths. For example, a good artist might be called Art; a horseshoe champ, Ringer or Champ; a basketball player, Wilt or Hoop; a physically strong boy, Bear; a person who likes gardening, Fleur, Violet, or Herb; a girl good in music, Melody.

Conduct a classroom discussion around the following questions: What are the names that would make you feel good—that would make you feel proud or self-confident? What are the names that make you feel bad—that make you lose your self-confidence? What would a classroom be like where everyone had a nickname that made him or her feel bad? What would a classroom be like if everyone had a nickname that made him feel good and self-confident?

Do you have any nicknames? How do they make you feel? What other names have you been called in your lifetime?

With older groups in high school you can have the class break into pairs. One at a time each student closes his eyes while his partner calls to him, repeatedly using one or more of his nicknames. Then the students can share the feelings evoked by the different names. These reactions should be recorded in their journals. This exercise can also be used as an introduction to writing poetry, short stories, etc.

We recently discovered a book entitled *The New Age Name Book* by Sue Browder (New York: Warner Paperback Library, 1974). It contains over 3,000 unusual, symbolic, and creative names not found in usual name books. You might ask students to find a new name that means something special to them. Some examples of girls names are Solana (Spanish for "sunshine"), Shani (Swahili for "marvelous"), Cari (Turkish for "flowing like water"), Tara ("Buddhist savior goddess"), Shaina (Yiddish for "beautiful"), Shashi (Japanese for "bliss"), Chenoa (North American Indian name meaning "white dove"). Boys' names include Ari (Hebrew for "lion"), Erin (Irish for "peace"), Kem (English gypsy name meaning "the sun"), Krispin (Slovakian for "curly-haired"), Manco (Inca name meaning "king"), Yuma (American Indian name meaning "son of a chief"), Dustin (German for "a fighter"), and Ragnar (Swedish meaning "mighty army"). This book can also be used for the exercise.

> *Healthy people, research shows, see themselves as liked, wanted, acceptable, able and worthy. Not only do they feel that they are people of dignity and worth, but they behave as though they were. Indeed, it is in this factor of how a person sees himself that we are likely to find the most outstanding differences between high and low self-image people. It is not the people who feel that they are liked and wanted and acceptable and able who fill our prisons and mental hospitals. Rather it is those who feel deeply inadequate, unliked, unwanted, unacceptable, and unable.*
>
> Donald E. Hamachek
> *Encounter with the Self*

45
what's in a name?

The purpose of this activity is to increase the student's self-concept through an understanding of his own names.

> What function do names serve? (They help us to identify and talk about specific individuals.)
>
> Who decides what name a person gets? (Parents)
>
> Where do parents get these names? (From their own names, from relatives, from books, from movies and television, from other people, etc.)

Names are passed down through history from one generation to another. At one time in history names actually had meanings. For example, first names like Philip meant "Lover of horses," Peter meant "rock or stone," Henry meant "home ruler," Edward meant "prosperous guardian," Margaret meant "a pearl," Judith meant "admired or praised," Ann (derived from Hannah) meant "full of grace, mercy, and prayer," and Shirley meant "from a white meadow."

Last names also had meaning. A "cooper" was a man who made barrels. A "smith" was a blacksmith, or one who worked with metal. A "miller" was one who ground grain, and a "potter" was a man who fashioned clay pottery.

Originally names were descriptive phrases to help identify people such as Philip, the cooper, or Peter, the smith. Eventually, the descriptive nouns came to stand for the people themselves—Philip Cooper and Peter Smith.

Using any of the readily available books of names, such as *4000 Names for Your Baby* (New York: Dell Publishing Co., 1962), allow the students to take turns looking up the meaning of their names and entering them in their journals. If a name is not listed, be sure to tell the student that it's because their name must be really special and suggest that they ask their parents for information on how their name was chosen or created.

> *For the potential of the oak lies vibrating within the atomic structure of the acorn, as does the flower live within the bud and the Self within man.*
>
> Master Subramuniya
> *Cognizantability*

Photo by Ginny Duff

46
positive feelings

Working with a small group or the whole class, ask the children to arrange their chairs in a circle so that everyone can see everyone else's face. Ask them to tell about something that makes them feel very good. You might first ask them to draw a picture or write a story about it and then share it in the circle.

A variation is to ask the children to share something they did that made someone else feel happy. You might start out by saying:

> Yesterday I told Jane that I liked the dress she was wearing. I thought the dress was very colorful. She smiled, and I think my comment made her feel good. Would you share with us something you have said or done for someone else that made him or her feel good? How did it make that person feel good?

Another variation is to ask the children to respond to the following instruction:

> Can you think of something that a grownup did or said to you this week that made you feel good? Could you share that thing with the group and tell us why it gave you a pleasant feeling?

This exercise could be used substituting teachers, best friends, pets, etc., for grownup. Some examples of past use of this exercise are:

> It made me feel good when the playground supervisor told one of the other kids to stop picking on me. I felt good because she noticed I was being hurt.
> I felt good when my mother said we could make cupcakes together and that I could bring them to school.

Doubts are more cruel
than the worst of truths.

Molière
Le Misanthrope

"I know that I am smart, as a matter of fact I am brilliant, I am great, In athletics the greatest, and the funny thing about this is that I am not conceited about it."

Lawrence Branagan and Christopher Moroney

47
COMMERCIAL FOR ONESELF

Methods of selling products are hardly foreign to this generation, but how many have ever considered advertising their own strengths and skills? As a self-enhancing activity tell the students they are going to spend the next several days making advertisements and commercials to sell themselves. They have the option of designing a magazine or newspaper advertisement, a poster, a billboard sign, a brochure, a radio or television commercial, or any other form of advertising they can think of (sweepstakes, coupons, etc.).

Allow several class periods for the students to develop their ideas and create their final product for display. You may wish to permit two or more students to work together in a team; for example, one student might be a good artist, another a good writer or photographer.

When students have completed their ads and commercials, take a period to share them all with the entire class. We suggest that contests, judging, and prizes be avoided; they only create unnecessary competition that can lead to feelings of inadequacy and resentment among those who do not win.

Materials needed: Poster paper, crayons, magic markers, water colors, brushes, scissors, magazines, newspapers, and paste. If available, typewriter, tape recorder, record player, records, videotape recorder, cameras, 8mm motion picture cameras, etc.

An optimist is wrong just about as often as a pessimist is, but the big difference is that he has a lot more fun.

Anonymous

48
positive
support techniques

Positive Feedback: At the end of a small-group session, students often wish to give each other some feedback or other data about themselves. Some beginning statements for giving feedback in a positive manner include:

I liked when you. . .   When you . . . I . . .
It helped me when you. . .   We were better as a group today because you . . .

Positive Support: Ask each student to list, and later to share, five things that another person can say, do, or recognize in them that makes them feel good or successful. For example:

1. Smile when you see me
2. Listen to me when I talk
3. Tell me that my contribution was useful

4. Hug or kiss me to show affection
5. Tell me that you missed me while I was gone

Positive Support Sharing: At some time during the week, suggest that the students make "I appreciate. . ." statements to each other. This can be done in the whole class, in small groups, or individually. This activity can encourage children to experiment, to take risks, and to try on new behaviors. It is important that you, as the teacher, model this "I appreciate. . ." behavior throughout the year. The exercise works best if you have each student share in turn around the room. This avoids the time delay and anxiety of waiting to see who goes next.

There is a need of staggering magnitude for doing something in our educational program to help children and youth acquire realistic attitudes of self-acceptance. A large proportion of the young people now entering adulthood are burdened with anxiety, hostility, defensiveness, attitudes toward themselves and others, feelings of guilt, inferiority, or other forms of self-disparagement and self-distrust. They struggle not only with the real dangers and thwartings in our troubled world but with unresolved childhood problems. They are beset with conflicts arising from unrealistic concepts and unhealthy attitudes which they carry from childhood into adult life.

Arthur T. Jersild
In Search of Self

"Who am I and where am I going?"

Henry Martin; © 1971 by Saturday Review/World

three
who am I ?

Ultimately, each of us is faced with three questions which we must answer in one way or another if we are to grow to greater personal maturity:

> Who Am I?
> Where Am I Going?
> Why?

Each of these questions, in its own way, deals with our sense of self, our goals, our values, our strengths and weaknesses, and our way of life or "life style." How we see ourselves and others is related to some extent in how we answer these three questions.[1]

With this paragraph Don Hamachek begins his excellent book *Encounter with the Self*. It is no accident that two of our sections are entitled "Who Am I?" and "Where Am I Going?"

In this particular section we again focus on the student's self-identity and the idea that "I'm glad I'm me!" We also use some of Sid Simon's valuing strategies to begin to get at Hamachek's third question, "Why?"

Don't feel that these exercises are so "heavy" that they might prove threatening to some students. Actually, our experience is that they continue to be fun. The insight that pupils get from doing these activities often comes from the discussion that follows quite naturally. Adults and teenagers especially benefit from talking it over after the exercises.

---

[1] Donald E. Hamachek, *Encounter with the Self* (New York: Holt, Rinehart and Winston, 1971)

ABOUT SCHOOL

Anonymous

This poem was handed to a grade 12 English teacher in Regina, Saskatchewan. Although it is not known if the student actually wrote it himself, it is known that he committed suicide two weeks later.

He always wanted to say things. But no one understood.
He always wanted to explain things. But no one cared.
So he drew.

Sometimes he would just draw and it wasn't anything. He wanted to carve it in stone or write it in the sky.

He would lie out on the grass and look up in the sky and it would be only him and the sky and the things inside that needed saying.

And it was after that, that he drew the picture. It was a beautiful picture. He kept it under the pillow and would let no one see it.

And he would look at it every night and think about it. And when it was dark, and his eyes were closed, he could still see it.

And it was all of him. And he loved it.

When he started school he brought it with him. Not to show anyone, but just to have it with him like a friend.

It was funny about school.

He sat in a square, brown desk like all the other square, brown desks and he thought it should be red.

And his room was a square, brown room. Like all the other rooms. And it was tight and close. And stiff.

He hated to hold the pencil and the chalk, with his arm stiff and his feet flat on the floor, stiff, with the teacher watching and watching.

And then he had to write numbers. And they weren't anything. They were worse than the letters that could be something if you put them together.

And the numbers were tight and square and he hated the whole thing.

The teacher came and spoke to him. She told him to wear a tie like all the other boys. He said he didn't like them and she said it didn't matter.

After that they drew. And he drew all yellow and it was the way he felt about morning. And it was beautiful.

The teacher came and smiled at him. "What's this?" she said. "Why don't you draw something like Ken's drawing?

Isn't that beautiful?"

It was all questions.

After that his mother bought him a tie and he always drew airplanes and rocket ships like everyone else.

And he threw the old picture away.

And when he lay out alone looking at the sky, it was big and blue and all of everything, but he wasn't anymore.

He was square inside and brown, and his hands were stiff, and he was like anyone else. And the thing inside him that needed saying didn't need saying anymore.

It had stopped pushing. It was crushed. Stiff.

Like everything else.

49
owl game

The old owl just sits there and repeats, "Who? Who? Who?" Maybe his "who" is not a question—but then, it might be. In the Owl Game the "owl" does ask a question, and asks it over and over. He asks his question with sincerity, empathy, and integrity. The respondent must trust his "owl" so he can say whatever pops into his mind. A long philosophical treatise is not an appropriate response; simply a word, phrase, or brief sentence will convey what the respondent is thinking at that moment.

This exercise seems to go better with students of high school age and over.

Ask the students to each find a partner—someone with whom they feel comfortable. Tell them to find a place to sit across from each other and to decide between them who is to be "A" and who is to be "B." After this has been determined, tell the A's that they can only ask the question "Who are you?" The B's, with their eyes closed, are to answer each time with a word or a short phrase. Ask them to continue this until you tell them to stop. Let them go at this in rapid-fire fashion for two to five minutes. Then have them switch roles with B asking "Who are you?" and A answering. Tell the students to say whatever comes into their heads, no matter how crazy, absurd or repetitive it may sound. If they don't, they'll get stuck. Next instruct the A's to ask the question, "Who do you pretend to be?" The B's are to answer as before. Again allow two to five minutes. Then have them switch roles again.

This exercise can be extended or repeated in a variation of this form by using the questions: "What do you want?" and "What are you feeling right now?"

We strongly advise you to allow time for discussion of this activity with the whole class reconvened. Discussion of personal results makes it possible for the students to become aware of both their unique and their common patterns of response. Tuning in to these patterns heightens one's self-awareness.

We learned this exercise from Bernard Gunther.

Researches I have conducted show that a person will permit himself to be known when he believes his audience is a man of goodwill.

Sidney M. Jourard

The Transparent Self

Photo by Ginny Duff

50

who am I questionnaire

Ask the children to fill out the following questionnaire. In order to assure that the students will be as open and honest as possible, you can tell them that the questionnaires will be kept confidential, unless the children wish to discuss the questions in small groups.

The questionnaire consists of the following incomplete sentences:

In general, school is. . .

This class is. . .

My best friend is. . .

The thing I like best about my class is. . .

Something I'd like to tell my teacher is. . .

I don't like people who. . .

I like people who. . .

I'm at my best when I. . .

Right now I feel. . .

People I trust. . .

The best thing that could happen to me is. . . .

When I don't like something I've done I. . .

When I like something I've done I. . .

When I'm proud of myself I. . .

I'm very happy that. . .

I wish my parents knew. . .

Someday I hope. . .

I would like to. . .

Five adjectives that describe me are. . .

Three things I want to become more of are. . .

To begin with, I've found that there is no one else like me, anywhere, like snowflakes. No one else feels completely the way I do. No one else sees things in the same scope as I do. So my first discovery about myself is that I'm me.

Quoted from a high school composition

51
voting...
& additional questions

It is necessary to discuss negative or "bad" feelings if one is to develop a healthy self-concept. if a child thinks some of his feelings of hostility, aggression, anger, and hate are unnatural or "bad," he will begin to perceive himself as bad or unnatural. Being able to talk about these feelings in the group has two positive effects on the child's self-image. First, it provides him with an opportunity to defuse some of the feelings by talking them out rather than acting them out in a potentially destructive way. Second, as a child sees that he is not the only one who sometimes wishes his older brother were dead or gets angry with his parents, he will see that his feelings are natural and common responses to similar emotional situations that he shares with his classmates. He will discover that it is acceptable to have these feelings—that it is "OK" to be the person he is.

To get at negative feelings, let students "vote" by raising their hands to indicate their experience with some of the following types of common childhood problems. Maintain an open and accepting environment of trust and empathy as you ask such questions as:

How many of you:

> Are afraid of ghosts?
> Ever get scared?
> Like to get angry?
> Are afraid when your parents get angry?
> Are afraid when your parents fight?
> Sometimes want to destroy everything in sight?
> Get so mad you could hit someone?
> Think you get bossed around too much at home; in school; by your friends; by grown-ups in general?
> Like one parent more than the other?

Use your creativity and experience to generate other questions, or ask your students to bring in their own lists of things that evoke negative feelings. Give them the opportunity to discuss any or all of these questions by simply asking, "Would anyone like to say anything about any of the questions?" That is usually all students need to get them into a lively discussion that fosters ventilation and reassurance as they see their feelings are common to others.

You might follow this up by having the children draw a picture of the event that caused the negative feeling to occur, by writing a story about the event, by role-playing or brainstorming alternative procedures for handling such events, and by setting goals to overcome, deal with, or avoid such situations in the future.

We have listed below some samples of other questions to give you an idea of the range of possibilities. Precede each question with a statement such as "How many of you. . ." or "How many here. . ."

Know what you want to do/be when you grow up?
Like to be teased? Sometimes tease others?
Are afraid of the dark? Of wild animals?
Think school is fun? Think school is hard?
Get spanked a lot?
Are the oldest child? The youngest? Middle? Only child?
Cry a lot?
Feel that life could be better for you?
Are in love right now? Wish you were in love right now?
Feel that life has not been fair to you?
Would like to change your name?
Feel happy most of the time?
Feel you have a communication problem with your parents?
Like one of your parents more than the other?
Feel closer to one of your parents than the other?
Get an allowance? Have to work for it?
Would like to change something about the way you look?
Have had a scary dream in the last month?
Have a lot of secrets that you keep?
Think people might not like you if they knew who you really were?
Think people *would* like you if they knew who you really were?
Don't like to talk in class?
Find it easy to make new friends?
Have been in a serious accident?
Have ever wanted to hurt someone for something they did to you?
Would rather be older or younger than you are right now?
Would like to live somewhere else?
Daydream sometimes?
Have had a tooth pulled?
Feel you have to work too hard?
Enjoy being outdoors more than being indoors?

These are just a few ideas to get you started. The best questions come from the concerns and interests of the students themselves. A great idea is to have students make up their own lists of questions and have them or you read it to the class.

Another excellent source of voting questions is the book *Values Clarification* by Sidney B. Simon, Leland Howe, and Howard Kirschenbaum (New York: Hart Publishing Co., 1972), available in paperback.

Adapted from Sidney B. Simon

. . .even the most insensitive parent or teacher can usually recognize and take into account a crippling physical handicap. Negative self-esteem, however, is often overlooked because we fail to take the time and effort it requires to be sensitive to how children see themselves and their abilities.

William W. Purkey
Self-Concept and School Achievement

Natural selection tells of limbs and functions which atrophy through lack of use; the power to feel, to experience and realize the precarious uniqueness of each other's being, can also wither in a society.

George Steiner
Encounter Magazine

52

the metaphor game

Divide your class into groups of five or six. Say, "In about a minute you are going to turn into an animal, a food, a car, and a color. Write down what you are going to turn into in each category. Don't think it up. Let what you are going to turn into emerge."

After everyone has written down a color, car, food, and animal for themselves, have them look around their group. "If you saw the members of your group turn into each of the four categories, what would you see? Write those down. If nothing comes to mind for a person in a category, skip it. Trust your first thought."

Now, the students should share what they have discovered by reading their own metaphors, then having the rest of the group share what they wrote for that person.

Come together with the whole group and share the experience and do some generalizing. A simple activity like this seems to lead people to question their patterns of perception and behavior, to speculate about alternative ways of behaving and, with encouragement, to experiment with some alternatives.

RED IS

Red is a fire jumping about.
Red is ketchup and sauerkraut.
Red is a picture on the wall.
Red is a carpet down the hall.
Red is a big beating heart.
Red is our chair that's falling apart.
Red is an apple on a tree.
And, when I'm real angry, red is me.

Anna Schneider

Photo by Ginny Duff

53

adjective wardrobe

Ask the students to tear a piece of paper into eight pieces. On each piece of paper they are to write one word which describes them. Remind them that because no one else will see the slips of paper, they should try to be as honest as possible. When they have completed this, have them arrange the papers in order, placing the one they are most pleased with at the top and the one they are least pleased with at the bottom.

Inform them that what they now have is a wardrobe of descriptive words that they can try on, wear, or discard. Ask them to consider one word at a time. Suggest that they spend a little time considering how they feel about each of the adjectives they have written down. Do they like it? Do they want to keep it? Expand it? Discard it or what?

Ask them to give up each quality one at a time. Do they feel naked? How are they changed? Ask them to fantasize what kind of person they would be with one, two, three, or all of these qualities removed. Have them reclaim the qualities one at a time. How do they feel now?

At the end of the exercise ask each student to record two things he has learned about himself. If there is time, ask the students to share their "I learned. . ." statements.

When a man no longer confuses himself with the definition of himself that others have given him, he is at once universal and unique.

Alan Watts
Psychotherapy East and West

"The trouble with you, Sheldon, is you lack self-confidence."

54

IF I WERE...

This activity is designed to help students clarify who they are, who they want to be, and what they want to do.

Working in groups of three, have the students share what they would be if they were suddenly turned into an animal, a bird, a car, a food, a flower, a musical instrument, or a building. This is usually a very enjoyable exercise, but it is essential that the students try to think of the best representations of their current personality. Ask them to share the reasons for their particular choice with their partners. For example:

> If I were a building, I'd be a small hut on a deserted island. I guess I feel that lonely sometimes.

> If I were a fruit, I'd be a pineapple because pineapples have a hard tough surface, but inside they are soft and sweet.

> If I were a bird, I'd be a canary because I like to sing a lot.

After several minutes of sharing such "If I were's" the class can be encouraged to consider "I would rather be. . ." statements. For example, the student who made the first statement above may add: "But I'd rather be a church so people could find peace in me!" "I would rather be. . ." statements indicate needs or strengths people would like to see actualized in themselves.

A major hang-up affecting educational change is the image we hold of ourselves. Too often we regard ourselves as incapable of effecting change and this apprehension keeps us locked in stereotyped shells incapable of displaying our real humanity. As we understand better the nature of change, we shall likely be unafraid to be genuine, authentic, and real human beings.
When this transformation takes place, as it must, we shall then be ready to face the realities involved in change with complete honesty. As real people, we shall learn to prize the learner—his feelings, his opinions, his person.
We shall then be able to admit and act upon our admission that it is caring for the learner that counts. Then it is that we shall be able to practice acceptance *as the most fundamental law underlying the learning process. Until we are committed to the belief that the other person is a somebody, not a nobody, and that somehow he is trustworthy—until this belief is actualized, we likely will have little interest in effecting worthwhile educational changes.*

Dr. A. Craig Phillips, North Carolina State Superintendent of Public Instruction

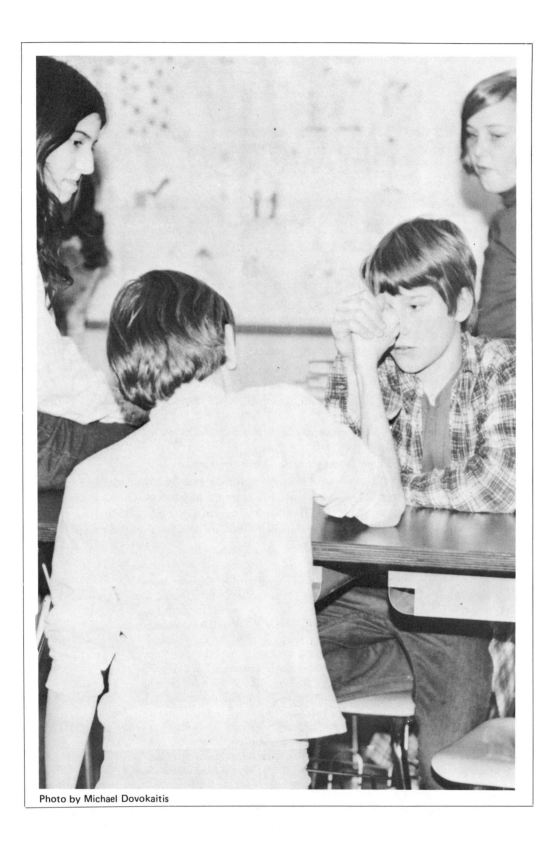

Photo by Michael Dovokaitis

55

if I could be...

This exercise is another way of helping students clarify who they are, what they want to be, and what they want to do. Have the students work in pairs and talk about their written responses to such questions as, "If I could be any animal (bird, insect, flower, food, etc.), I'd be an _____ because. . . ." This done, have them form larger groups to share their choices and reasons. Here are some ideas to start with.

If I could be any animal, I'd be a(n) ____ because. . .
If I could be a bird, I'd be a(n) ____ because. . .
If I could be an insect, I'd be a(n) ____ because. . .
If I could be a flower, I'd be a(n) ____ because. . .
If I could be a tree, I'd be a(n) ____ because. . .
If I could be a piece of furniture, I'd be a(n) ____ because. . .
If I could be a musical instrument, I'd be a(n) ____ because. . .
If I could be a building, I'd be a(n) ____ because. . .
If I could be a car, I'd be a(n) ____ because. . .
If I could be a street, I'd be ____ because. . .
If I could be a state, I'd be ____ because. . .
If I could be a foreign country, I'd be ____ because. . .
If I could be a game, I'd be ____ because. . .
If I could be a record, I'd be ____ because. . .
If I could be a TV show, I'd be ____ because. . .
If I could be a movie, I'd be ____ because. . .
If I could be a food, I'd be ____ because. . .
If I could be a part of speech, I'd be a(n) ____ because. . .
If I could be any color, I'd be ____ because. . .

The teacher as a person is more important than the teacher as a technician.
What he is has more effect than anything he does.

Jack Canfield

"I AM HAVING A REAL SELF IMAGE PROBLEM
... MY COMPUTER KEEPS CALLING ME BY
THE WRONG NUMBER ...."

Short and Weaver Cartoons

56

what if...

This exercise helps students (and you) become aware of what feelings they have about themselves through the use of projection. It often turns out that even children who do not feel appreciated by people will often project a deeper sense of self-appreciation into the objects discussed in the exercise.

Start the exercise with comments and questions such as:

> Did you ever think of things like "What if my bike could talk?" What do you think your bicycle would say about you? Pretend you are something on this list, and tell us what it would say about you.

Toothbrush	Baseball glove	Dresser	Radio	Brush	Doll
Bed	Schoolbus	Dog	School desk	Coat	
Shoes	Closet	Television set	Refrigerator	Hat	

Have the students verbally share their responses or write their responses as a composition or in their journals. A variation would be to have the students talk about themselves as they imagine their mother, father, brother, sister, teacher, best friend, pet, etc., would talk about them. This variation requires a higher level of trust and openness.

Our experience is that these exercises work best with highly verbal children from about fourth grade up.

Idea by Doris Shallcross

A student was asked if he ever got the feeling that studying at a machine is too impersonal. "No. It doesn't make you feel inferior. The teachers always make you feel, 'Man, I'm three pegs above you.' You can turn off a machine that quick, but you can't shut up a teacher."

A black student commented: "What I like about the machine is that it doesn't know I'm black."

Bernard Asbell
Think Magazine

I Used to...But Now

OSCAR MARCILLA

I used to be liked by every girl in my class
    but now only a few like me.
I used to be an astronaut but now I'm not because
I ate too much moon cheese and I can't fit in the
    rocket ship.
I used to make people but now I make animals.
I used to like pancakes but now I like
    handcakes
(A handcake is what your hand is after it got
    stepped on.)
I used to have a birthday, but now, I eat too
    much so it's a burpday.
I used to jump from 500 feet, but now I jump
    from 499 feet and 11 inches.
I used to eat dogs in the winter, but now I eat
    hot-dogs in the summer.
I used to eat food when I was hungry but now I
    eat Turkey.

57

I USED TO BE...
BUT NOW I'M...

Ask the group to sit in a circle. Begin this exercise by saying:
I always used to (pause), but now I'm (pause). Can you think of something
you used to be or do or think that has changed?

If the statements are incomplete, ask them to make them more complete. For instance,
if a student says, "I used to be happy but now I'm not," you should respond, "You
used to be happy but now you're not what?"

Examples of student responses have been:

I used to be worried about someone stealing my bank, but now I'm not worried.
I used to worry about having awful penmanship, but now I'm working harder.
I used to be afraid of the dark, but now my mother can shut the door.
I used to be afraid of the witch at the Halloween party but now I'm not afraid.

An adaptation of this exercise is to have the students write their responses in sentence
form on paper. These are handed in and the teacher reads them in random order, thus
forming a poem written by the entire class. This can later by typed up and posted or
distributed to the students.

For other creative poetry and self-awareness exercises see *Wishes, Lies, and Dreams:
Teaching Children to Write Poetry*, by Kenneth Koch (New York: Random House,
1971). Also contact the Teachers and Writers Collaborative, 244 Vanderbilt Avenue,
Brooklyn, New York 11205.

> *So, we are understanding today that human intelligence can be created, that it
> is a function of the richness and the extent and the availability of perceptions.
> This, of course, is determined in very large part by the self-concept. How you
> perceive yourself determines what you think you are able to do and that
> determines in turn what you will try. So the self-concept has a tremendous
> effect upon the intelligence of the individual.*
>
> Arthur W. Combs
> *Perceiving, Behaving, and Becoming*

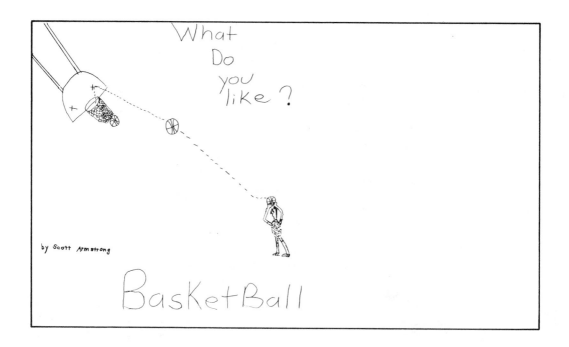

What
Do
you
like ?

by Scott Armstrong

BasketBall

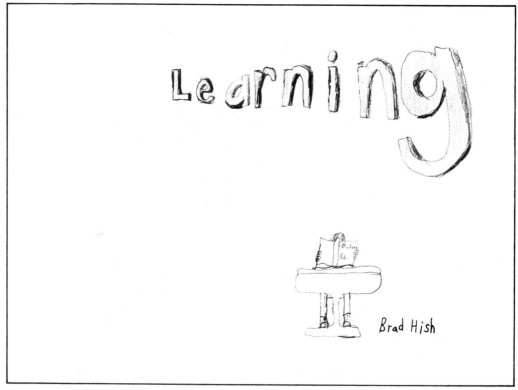

Learning

Brad Hish

58

twenty
things I like to do

Ask each student to number a sheet of paper from 1 to 20 (see p. 134). Then ask them to list twenty things they like to do in whatever order the activities occur to them.

When they have completed this, ask them to annotate each item with the following codes:

Put a dollar sign ($) next to each item that cost over five dollars every time you do it.

Place a *P* next to each item that you enjoy more when you are doing it with somebody, and an *A* next to those things you enjoy more when you are doing it along.

Put a *PI* next to each activity that requires planning.

Beside each activity, place the date when you did it last, if you can remember.

Place an *F* or *M* next to each item you think your father or mother would have listed when they were your age.

Place an * next to each item you would want your future wife or husband to have on their list. For example:

1.	Go surfing	P, Pl,	8/5/70		
2.	Play basketball	P, Pl,	9/27/70,	F	
3.	Dance	P,	3/38/71,	M	*
4.	Read poetry		3/25/71		
5.	Go to the movies	$, P, Pl,	2/31/71,	F	

When the students have completed the coding, ask them to make a few "I learned. . ." statements (see Exercise 1). Statements made by students in the past include "I learned I don't need money to be happy." "I learned I like things better when they are spontaneous." "I learned I need to plan more." "I learned I haven't done the things I like to do for a long time."

This would be an opportune time to introduce the concept of goal-setting. Students could be asked to set a goal to do something they like to do, but that they haven't done for a long time (see Exercise 86).

Exercise by Sidney B. Simon

The thing that keeps people from becoming enlightened is that they believe they don't deserve it.

	$	P/A	P1	F/M	*	date	You can invent other codes.		
1									
2									
3									
4									
5									
6									
7									
8									
9									
10									
11									
12									
13									
14									
15									
16									
17									
18									
19									
20									

I learned that I _____

59

who are we?

Ask the students to sit in a circle with you. Start the discussion by asking the question:

> Who are we? How would you answer that question if a Martian were to ask that of us, right now, as we sit here in our circle?

This exercise has been used very successfully with elementary school students. Some examples of what they have said are:

> We are human beings. We can think, talk, and do stuff.
> We are people who can move and think, but we can't make magic.
> We are different from each other.

They never once mentioned that they were "children" or "young people"!

High school students and college students can handle this exercise profitably as well. After the group seems to have exhausted the "Who are we?" question you may want to switch your focus to an individual (with his or her permission, of course). (See Exercise 62.)

> *"I wonder if I've been changed in the night?"* [asks Alice] *"Let me think: was I the same when I got up this morning? I almost think I can remember feeling a little different. But if I'm not the same, the next question is 'Who in the world am I?' Ah,* that's *the great puzzle!"*
>
> Lewis Carroll
> *Alice in Wonderland*

UPI Photo

60

one of a kind

Start by creating a piece of "art" in front of the class. Don't worry about the quality of the finished product—the uniqueness of the creation is what counts. If you are "uptight" about this, practice once ahead of time. All you need is a piece of drawing paper and several colors of crepe paper and a stapler or some paste.

Get the children's attention and then proceed to tear various colors of crepe paper into jagged free-form patterns which you then mount on the drawing paper. You may make a "picture," but you'd probably be better off to create a simple design or an abstract expression. It should only take five minutes or less to put together something reasonably attractive and unique. Talk to the class and have fun while you're working (be a ham!). When you've finished your masterpiece, ask:

> Have you ever seen this before? One *exactly* like this? What things can you say about this "work of art" that are true? Do you know the meaning of any of these words—"creation," "creative," "create," "creatively"?

Lead the children to discuss the fact that what you did was create a piece of art. It would be impossible to duplicate the exact creation because the same tears in the paper could not be made, the same paper could not be used, etc. A "picture" that *looks* like yours could be constructed but it would not be the same work of art.

After you have completed the discussion, ask the children to create their own "masterpieces." Permit them to choose between using crepe paper, construction paper, crayons, or magic markers. Allow about five to ten minutes for this. When the students have completed their creations, ask them to compare them with each others'. Ask if any are the same. They should realize that each work of art is one of a kind.

When they pretty well understand what you're talking about, you should ask:

> Can any of these same ideas we've talked about be applied to human beings?

Again, lead them to a gradual realization through their own thinking that each of them is different, each unique, each irreplaceable and impossible to duplicate.

> *To be nobody-but-myself—in a world which is doing its best, night and day, to make you everybody else—means to fight the hardest battle which any human being can fight, and never stop fighting.*
>
> e. e. cummings
>
> *e. e. cummings—a miscellany*

61

who's who

Appoint several students to compile a *Who's Who in the Class*. Data can be gathered such as achievements, hobbies, pets, future aspirations, home addresses, family members. and "favorites," such as favorite TV program, favorite food, etc. When the data is collected and written up, see if you can have it duplicated and distributed to all the students.

If facilities are available, pictures can also be used. In addition to publishing a *Who's Who*, you could also have the data posted on a corridor bulletin board to share the information with the rest of the school.

We learn through experience and experiencing, and no one teaches us anything. If the environment permits it, anyone can learn what he chooses to learn; and if the individiual permits it, the environment will teach him everything it has to teach.

Viola Spolin
Improvisation for the Theater

62

weekly reaction sheets

Part of enhancing a student's self-concept is helping him become more aware of the control he actually has over his daily life. Weekly reaction sheets help students see how effectively they are using their time.

Hand out a sheet with the following questions:

Name_____ Date_____

1. What was the high point of the week?
2. Whom did you get to know better this week?
3. What was the major thing you learned about yourself this week?
4. Did you institute any major changes in your life this week?
5. How could this week have been better?
6. What did you procrastinate about this week?
7. Identify three decisions or choices you made this week. What were the results of these choices?
8. Did you make any plans this week for some future event?
9. What unfinished personal business do you have left from this last week? How long have you been carrying it? How long do you plan to carry it?
10. Open comment:

At the end of a six-week period, you should return the reaction sheets to the students. Students may volunteer to talk about any or all of the questions. Ask them to try to summarize any patterns they can discern in their responses to the questions. Ask them to make a series of "I learned. . ." statements after their review of their sheets.

After one six-week period has elapsed, we find it interesting and profitable to have the students construct a new weekly reaction sheet based on what they feel are important areas to be examined in their lives.

> *Every teacher is in his own way a psychologist. Everything he does, says, or teaches has or could have a psychological impact. What he offers helps children to discover their resources and their limitations. He is the central figure in countless situations which can help the learned to realize and accept himself or which may bring humiliation, shame, rejection, and self-disparagement.*
>
> Arthur T. Jersild
> *In Search of Self*

63

PUBLIC INTERVIEW

This method of enhancing self-concept has great possibilities, but it should be used with caution; the classroom climate should be friendly, warm, and accepting before it is used.

The purpose of the public interview is to gain a deeper knowledge of the student, to give the student the opportunity to publicly receive the attention of all his classmates, to suggest life alternatives to others, and to show the students that they are not alone in many of the feelings they have.

Ask for a volunteer to be interviewed in public. The selected student is asked to stand in front of the class. A series of questions (appropriate to the age level) is asked. The student may choose to answer the questions or to "pass." It is important that the right to pass is made explicit.

The interview may be terminated at any time by either of the participants, especially the student being interviewed. A simple statement like "Thank you for the questions" automatically brings the interview to a stop.

At the end of the interview, the student may ask the interviewer any of the same questions that were asked him. Interview information may be recorded and used as a page for the student's journal.

Some sample interview questions are:

1. What is your favorite sport?
2. What do you like best about school? Least about school?
3. What kind of TV programs do you like to watch?
4. What would you do with $1000?
5. If you were a teacher, how would you teach your class?
6. Do you have a hobby that takes up a lot of your time? What is it? How did you get interested in it?
7. What is your idea of a perfect Saturday afternoon?
8. What changes would you make to improve the school?
9. Have you ever invented anything? What?
10. What is the best news you could get now?

11. Is there something you want badly but can't afford right now?
12. Do you work after school or on the weekends? Where? What are you using the money for?
13. If you had three wishes, what would they be?
14. What is the best thing that ever happened to you?
15. Can you think of something you would be willing to say to the class that you think might be good for them to hear?

This exercise is taken from *About Me: Teacher's Guide* by Harold Wells and Jack Canfield, available from Encyclopedia Britannica Educational Corporation, 425 North Michigan Avenue, Chicago, Illinois 60611. Originally developed by Louis E. Raths, Merrill Harmin, and Sidney B. Simon and can be found in greater detail in their book *Values and Teaching* (Columbus, Ohio: Charles E. Merrill, 1966), pp. 142-49.

Photo by Vinnie Scarano

64

the public statement

Whenever it is requested, allow students a short period of time, say five minutes, to make a public statement to the class. This could be done any time there is an extra five minutes available. The student's statement should be about something that he wants to say to his classmates. It may be a statement of criticism or of public affirmation. It may be highly emotional or extremely objective. In any case, it comes solely from the student and is not to be censored or countered by the teacher or the rest of the class. It is to be a public statement without rebuttal. Other students may wish to react at a later date with statements of their own addressed to the same topic, but a debate should not be allowed to develop.

If one's self-concept is to grow, he must have the opportunity to publicly affirm the things he believes in. This experience also provides the student with temporary control over his environment, for during the public statement he has control of all the ears in the room; those precious few moments are his and his alone. The public statement also indicates to the class that the teacher respects student ideas.

As an alternative, ask the students to submit opinion papers on whatever they would care to voice an opinion about. Opinion papers might be submitted as a reaction to someone else's public statement. These papers should not be corrected or graded.

A circus owner bought a most remarkable crow. Next night, his wife told him that she had cooked it. "Cooked it!" howled the owner. "Good grief, that bird could speak eight languages!" "So," shrugged the wife, "why didn't it say something?"

Burk Uzzle from Magnum Photos

65

motorcycle fantasy

In several places in this book we've used different mental images or fantasies to help a student get some insight into his personality. This is another such exercise. It has special appeal to older children and youth because motorcycling is currently so popular with them.

Prepare your class for a brief fantasy experience. The children should be relaxed, happy, sitting with their eyes closed. Speak softly but clearly and pause briefly between sentences so they have time to visualize your directions.

> Imagine that you are a motorcycle. Notice what kind you are and what make. You are being ridden now. Notice who your rider is. How do you get along with each other? Have a dialogue with your rider; finish the dialogue and become aware of how fast you are going. Notice where you are. What kind of condition are you, the motorcycle, in? Notice all of your various parts. Is everything working smoothly? Any badly worn parts about to cause trouble? Where are you now? Notice how you feel being a motorcycle. Your left handlebar has a brake grip for the front wheel and your right handlebar has the acceleration grip. Carry on a dialogue or conversation between the front wheel brake grip on the left and the accelerator on the right. Notice carefully what each is saying and feeling. You are being stopped now. Where did you stop and how? How do you feel after your ride?

Break the students into groups of three or four to discuss their experiences. The fantasy usually leads to an animated discussion. Don't interpret or suggest "good" and "bad" concerning any fantasy content. Let your students take what they can from the activity without pressing for insight.

This particular fantasy was suggested by John O. Stevens and is included in his excellent book *Awareness,* which is a collection of Gestalt awareness exercises.

Anything you can do to increase communication in your class will reduce your need to impose order by authority, and reduce the student's need to rebel against that authority. The class will become more a place for listening and learning, and less a place for fighting and antagonism.

John O. Stevens
Awareness

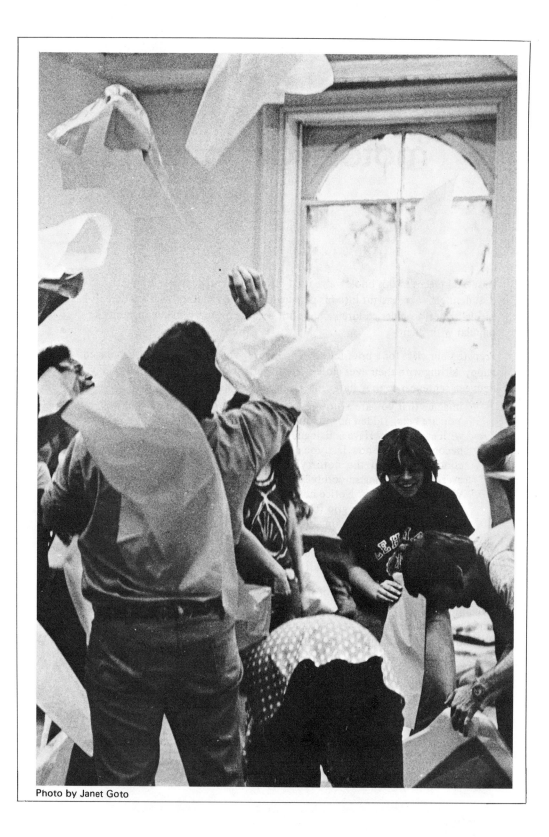

Photo by Janet Goto

four
accepting my body

There is an accumulating literature concerning the body and emotions. There has also been a recent emergence of body therapies such as bioenergetics, structural integration (Rolfing), psychomotor therapy, movement therapy, dance therapy, yoga, acupuncture, Feldenkrais movement, polarity therapy, massage therapy, etc. All these approaches stress the importance of body awareness for the development and maintenance of a strong self-concept. Alexander Lowen has written,

> The feeling of identity stems from a feeling of contact with the body. To know who one is, an individual must be aware of what he feels. He should know the expression on his face, how he holds himself, and the way he moves. Without this awareness of bodily feeling and attitude, a person becomes split into a disembodied spirit and a disenchanted body.[1]

In this section we have included a variety of different kinds of exercises. The first are simply some warm-up games which involve body movement and body contact. They can be used anytime with almost any age group. In the second group there are exercises aimed at helping students to achieve a clearer sense of their physical *appearance*. Third, there are exercises designed to relax body tension, to heighten sensory awareness, and to develop sensitivity to body messages.

---

[1] Alexander Lowen, *The Betrayal of the Body* (New York: Macmillan, 1967).

66

baker's dozen

1. *Records:* Have each student bring in the record that most symbolizes who he is or how he feels. Play the record for the rest of the class. Discuss the words and rhythm and the students' reactions.

2. *The Perfect Age:* Have the students write an essay on the topic "The Perfect Age." Have a discussion afterward.

3. *Ten Minute Break:* Give your students at least a ten-minute break during the day. Emphasize that this ten minutes is theirs to be used in whatever manner they choose. This period should not be used as a reward or a punishment—just let it happen. Report to the class afterward on your observations. Do the students agree?

4. *Personalized Space:* Have the students bring in material to decorate their own desks. For example, cloth, leather, or a flour sack can be used as a seat cover. Solicit other ways that they might personalize their study areas, lockers, etc.

5. *What It's Like To Be Me:* Write and deliver a short speech on "What It's Like To Be Me." That should turn the kids on to wanting to do the same—let them.

6. *Writing:* Have older students (8 to 14 years) prepare readers (using stories they make up, and based on their vocabulary studies of early grade books) for youngsters in earlier grades.

7. *"Me" Poem:* Have the students write a poem entitled: "Me!"

8. *Names for Spelling:* Use students' first and last names as part of the spelling lists during the first weeks of school. This is especially useful in urban schools, where there is such a variety of names.

9. *Mirrors:* Have mirrors in class where children can observe themselves. You can also have them role-play dialogues with themselves in the mirror, describe what they see in the mirror, etc.

10. *Love:* Have students write an essay on how they experience (give and receive) love.

11. *Physical Appearance:* Have the students discuss which things about their physical appearance it is possible to change and which things it is necessary to accept. Where did they get their ideas of good looks?

12. *Smile Break:* When there seems to be an undue amount of tension or anxiety in the classroom, you can defuse the situation by calling for a "smile break" with the words "Let's take thirty seconds for a smile break" or "Any volunteers for a smile?"

13. *Laughter:* Ask all the students to close their eyes and relax as much as possible. When this is achieved ask everybody to start laughing as loud as they can, and then you start laughing. They will all join in and soon it will become contagious, natural, spontaneous laughter. It's fun!

67

some body games

RAG DOLL—TIN SOLDIER

This exercise loosens people up by having them make contact with each other in a playful way. Ask the students to choose partners of approximately the same physical size. When they are in pairs, ask them to designate themselves A and B. Tell them that in the first round A's will be tin soldiers and B's will be their directors. Tin soldiers can only move forward. They have no power to think or make decisions. Demonstrate for the students how a tin soldier walks: slowly, with stiff legs and arm joints—like a toy tin solider. Then tell them that B's job is to guide his tin soldier and to turn him so as to avoid hitting walls, tables, and other tin soldiers walking around the room. Now have the B's wind up their tin soldiers and turn them on. Things often get quite rambunctious in this exercise, but as long as things don't get too chaotic, let it happen. The students enjoy it!

After a few minutes, stop the action and have them reverse roles so that B is now the tin soldier with A leading. Again after a few minutes, stop them and give them these new instructions.

A's are to be on their backs on the floor. They are to become totally limp, like rag dolls. B's job is to stand them up. It is an almost impossible task if the A's remain limp. The exercise is a lot of fun. Again after a few minutes, reverse roles.

After all segments of the exercise have been completed, bring the students together in a circle and ask them to share what that was like for them. Ask questions such as: How did you feel? Was it fun? What did you do? What were you thinking about when you were the leader? Was it easier to be the tin soldier or the leader? Was it frustrating trying to stand your rag doll up? As you get into this, you'll find that more questions will come to mind. If nobody has much of anything to say, that's OK, too. Remember this is just a warm up, so simply go on to another exercise.

FREEZE TAG

This exercise works best in a large group. Arbitrarily designate about one-fourth to one-third of the group as "it." This can be done by designating all those wearing the color red, or tennis shoes, or those over ten years of age, or whatever. These are the "freezers." Their task is to freeze the rest of the group. They do this by tagging someone and yelling "Freeze!" The person tagged must stop and freeze in his position at the time he is tagged. Although this sounds simple, the catch is that anyone still unfrozen may unfreeze a frozen member by touching him and yelling "Unfreeze." The game is a lot of fun and generates a lot of energy. It is good for a sleepy group and can be played with as many as 100 people in a gymnasium.

THE HUMAN PRETZEL

Ask for someone in the class who likes to solve puzzles. Send that person out of the room or into a corner with his eyes closed for a minute. The rest of the class joins hands in a circle. Then, without breaking the hand contact, they tangle themselves up by going under, over, in, and out of each other's arms. When the class is thoroughly entangled, ask the detective to return and try to untangle the group by giving verbal instructions to different people as to how they should move.

STATUES

Ask the students to choose partners, and have them designate themselves A and B. A's are to be sculptors and B's are to be clay. A's job is to mold B into a statue that expresses how he (A) is feeling right now. When this is done (allow a few minutes), ask the B's to tell the A's how they imagine they must be feeling. Give them a few minutes for sharing and then reverse the process.

MIRRORING

Have the class stand in two evenly matched rows, both facing the same direction (with one student standing in back of another student). Have the students in the front row begin to move their whole bodies, including their arms and their legs. Have the students in the back row try to exactly copy every move of the student directly in front of him. Allow about three to four minutes for this.

Now have all the children turn and face the opposite direction. Repeat as above, having the students in the front row move and the students in the back row copy. Again allow about three minutes for this.

Explain to the students that this is called "mirroring." Take a few minutes to talk about a real mirror and what happens when we look into one.

Now have the students face each other. Have one be the "Mirror," the one who copies exactly, and the other the "doer," the one who controls the mirror's actions. Allow about three minutes for this. Then change roles and allow another three minutes. Encourage the students to use their whole body, including facial expressions. Suggest that they can try to turn around together, move about in the room, jump up and down, etc.

After the exercise is over, ask the students to talk about which role was easier for them— leading or following. With older students you can ask them to think about what the world would be like if everyone always wanted to lead and there were no followers, or vice versa. How might their individual preference for leading or following affect their behavior in the class? What is dificult about leading (being judged, feeling the pressure to be creative or funny, feeling awkward, etc.) and about following (giving up my control to another person, feeling inferior, not doing it well, being asked to do some movement that isn't comfortable, etc.)? What are the advantages of leading and of following? How do they feel when they are dancing and they are the leader or the follower? Do they make up steps or imitate others?

We learned this particular version of the mirroring exercise from Gloria Castillo. We recommend her book *Left-Handed Teaching* (New York: Praeger, 1974).

68

STUDENT PHOTOGRAPHS

Many students will have photographs of themselves from home, school, dime-store booths, etc. If enough students have these pictures, they can be mounted on different-colored construction paper and placed on a bulletin board with interesting biographical material included.

If pictures are not readily available, you may want to take pictures of the students with an Instamatic or Polaroid Camera. Both cameras are available at minimal cost or can be borrowed.

A variation of this activity is to compare students' baby pictures with their current photos. If enough baby pictures are available, it is fun to have the class try to guess the identity of the person in each picture. This variation reinforces the fact that everyone has distinct features and unique characteristics, as well as illustrates the concept of change and growth.

A friend of mine traveling in Mexico saw a beautiful child and asked permission of the mother to photograph him. She was pleased by the request but when the photographer was leaving she stopped him and said, "Touch him," and then she added, "A child that is not touched will be unlucky."

Laura Huxley
You Are not the Target

69

fingerprints

The purpose of this activity is to demonstrate that everyone is unique and different in many ways—one of which is their fingerprints.

Have the children divide themselves into groups of five and supply each group with an ink pad. After cautioning them about getting ink on their clothing, ask them to make their fingerprints by first pressing their fingers on an ink pad and then on a sheet of white paper. The best print is obtained by rolling the finger from left to right without squeezing down too hard. Using magnifying glasses, have them carefully study and compare each others' prints.

After they have done this, ask the children if they have any ideas of how policemen use fingerprints to catch criminals. Everyone's fingerprints are unique and different. They can be used to identify one another.

THE BEGINNING TEACHER

Greeting his pupils, the master asked:
   "What would you learn of me?"
And the reply came:
   "How shall we care for our bodies?"
   "How shall we rear our children?"
   "How shall we work together?"
   "How shall we live with our fellow man?"
   "How shall we play?"
And the teacher pondering these words sadly walked away, for his own learning touched not these things.

Source Unknown

70

mirror mirror

Bring a full-length mirror to class. (Very usable full-length mirrors can be purchased at most discount or variety stores for very little money.) It is best if you can mount the mirror somewhere in the room so that it can be there permanently. The following are a few things that you can do with the mirror.

Start by having one student at a time (working in small groups or in the total classroom group) look into the mirror and tell what he sees. You can facilitate the process by asking such questions as:

> Close your eyes, open them, look quickly into the mirror, and tell what you see first.
>
> As you look at yourself in the mirror, tell what you like best.
>
> If the mirror could talk to you, what do you think it would say?
>
> What doesn't the mirror know about you?

Participation in this procedure sometimes takes a lot of courage. Often students will find it difficult to say anything positive about the image of themselves they see in the mirror. It is important, therefore, that you encourage positive expression by pointing out things that *you* see in them. The results of this exercise are well worth the effort.

Another exercise is to have a student volunteer give himself a strength bombardment (see Exercise 40) using the mirror. Ask him to pick five people he likes and knows well. They are to stand behind him as he sits in front of the mirror. They should stand in such a way so that he is able to see all of their faces in the mirror. The volunteer is then to look at himself in the mirror, maintaining eye contact with himself at all times, and tell himself positive things about himself—nothing else, just the positives! The five people standing behind him are to feed him positive things to say to himself whenever he gets stuck, yet they should not rush in too fast. Leaving a little space between inputs allows the volunteer the opportunity to call upon his own inner resources for evoking positive data about himself. Allow about five minutes for this exercise.

The mirror can also be used to facilitate discussions between black and white children. You might have two children (one white and one black) stand in front of the mirror together and ask them questions such as "How are you alike and different from each other in the mirror? Tell what you see about the other person. Tell something about yourself that the mirror doesn't know. Tell something about the other person that the mirror doesn't know. Does the mirror show what people are like on the inside?"

> Just go to the mirror and look at yourself
> And see what the man has to say;
> For it isn't your father, or mother, or wife,
> Who judgment upon you must pass.
> The fellow whose verdict counts most in your life
> Is the one staring back from the glass.
>
> Author unknown

71

the trust walk

This exercise is best done after students have gotten to know each other fairly well. It greatly adds to the level of trust and closeness in a class.

Ask the students to pick a partner they feel friendly with or close to. (After the initial exposure to this exercise, you can have them pick partners with people they feel that they don't know very well.) Tell them that they will be going on a walk together in which one person will have his eyes closed and the other will be guiding him. Ask them to decide who would like to be the first with their eyes closed. When they have decided, tell them that the guide's job is to make sure that their partner is safe at all times—i.e., doesn't bump into anything or fall down the stairs. The guides should also try to give their partner as interesting a walk as possible. They can take their partners up and down stairs, into places that have different noises, walk them backwards, run and jump with them, go in circles, etc. They can also give their partner a variety of different sensory experiences by placing their hands on objects with different textures such as smooth glass, rough concrete, a soft carpet, a water fountain, a pile of towels, a fur coat, the keys of a piano, etc. Ask them to use their ingenuity and imagination.

Tell them that this entire exercise is to be done without talking. Both partners are to be silent the whole time. After about ten or fifteen minutes, using a prearranged signal (a bell, a record player, a trumpet blast, etc.), have them switch roles. After another ten to fifteen minutes, have them return to the group and share their experiences. You can facilitate the discussion with such questions as:

> Were you able to trust your partner with your eyes closed?
> Did you open your eyes at any time?
> Did you find it easier following or leading? What was easy or hard about it?
> Did you enjoy the exercise? What did you enjoy about it?

Trust is the result of a risk successfully survived.

Jack R. Gibb

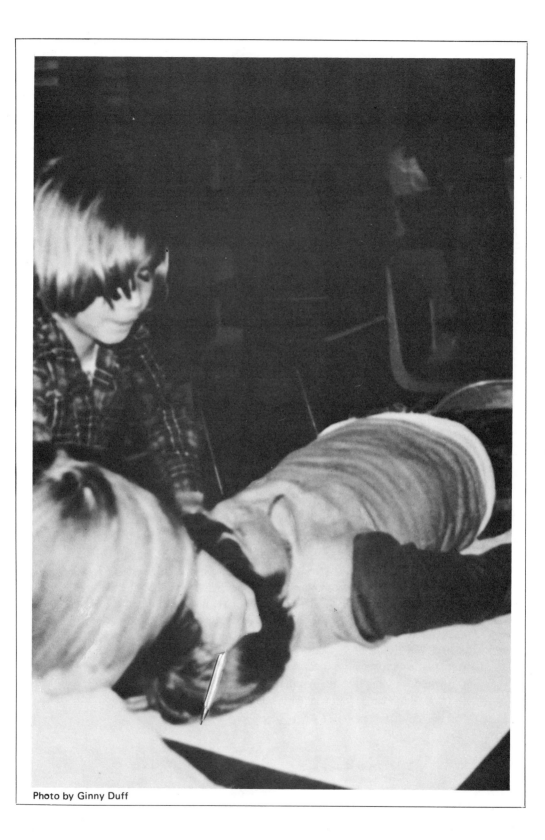

Photo by Ginny Duff

72

body tracing

Ask the students to form pairs. Have each student lie down on a piece of heavy brown wrapping paper while his partner traces an outline of his body. The students can then cut the figures out and color them.

This provides a life-sized self-portrait for each child. When the pictures are completed, the teacher can put them up around the room for display.

You may wish to keep the pictures, repeat the exercise at the end of the year, and have the class compare their new figures with their earlier productions.

To add to the impact of this exercise, ask each child to write a short story describing himself entitled "This Is Me." Tape these stories onto the hands of the students' self-portraits.

> *Each human being is born as something new, something that never existed before. He is born with what he needs to win at life. Each person in his own way can see, hear, touch, taste, and think for himself. Each has his own unique potentials—his capabilities and limitations. Each can be a significant, thinking, aware, and creatively productive person in his own right—a winner.*
>
> Muriel James and Dorothy Jongeward
> *Born to Win: Transactional Analysis with Gestalt Experiments*

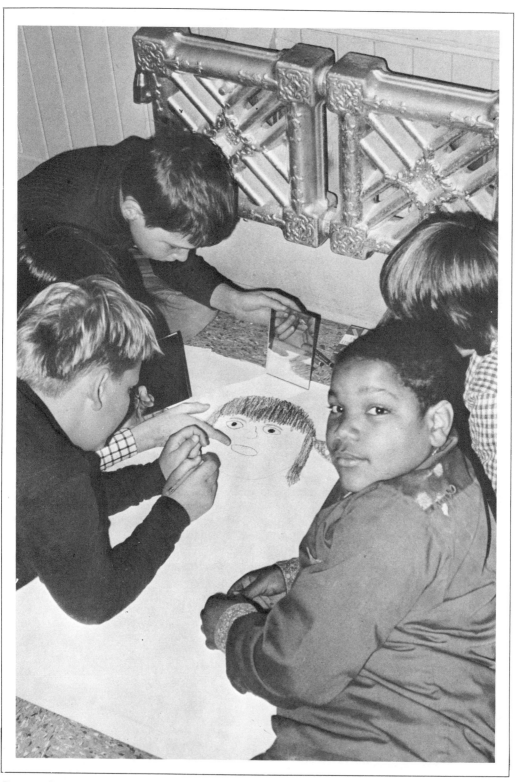

Photo by Ginny Duff

73
composite picture

Have your class get into groups of five or six. Tell each group that they are to draw a picture of an imaginary person. This person will be a composite of the best features of each of the members of their group. Great artistry is not needed in this exercise because the important notion is to get the group members to seek the pleasing features of the other members of the group. You might suggest some parts of the composite—head shape, hairline, hair color, eyes, ears, etc.—or have the class first brainstorm as many physical characteristics as they can think of and list them on the blackboard. Once the first choice is made, the rest of the exercise falls into place and a warm experience is usually had by everyone. It is also fun to display the portraits to the rest of the class and identify the features. Attention can be focused on the way participants felt before the exercise and the way they feel afterward.

The exercise increases the students' awareness of each other because permission is given by the exercise to look closely at the other group members. The activity may draw students closer together in a more mutually satisfying relationship.

You may find that an actual drawing is unnecessary. Just deciding which physical characteristics of each person would be chosen is enough to get the idea across.

This exercise was developed by Gerald Weinstein.

A survey of college co-eds showed that 90% were dissatisfied in some way with their appearance. If the words "normal" or "average" mean anything at all, it is obvious that 90% of our population cannot be "abnormal" or "different" or "defective" in appearance. Yet, similar surveys have shown that approximately the same percentage of our general population find some reason to be ashamed of their body-image.

Maxwell Maltz
Psycho-Cybernetics

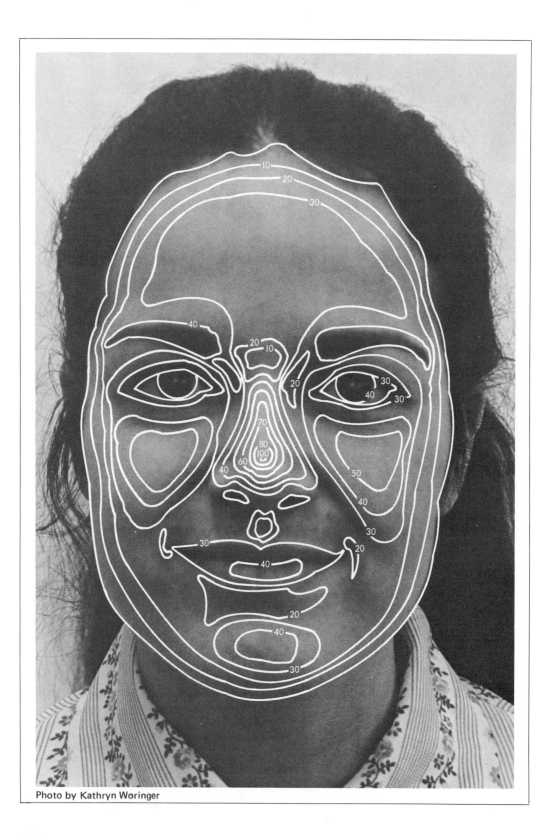

Photo by Kathryn Woringer

74

GEOGRAPHY OF THE SELF

This is great introspective material for older students' journals. Have the students consider the following questions about themselves in geographical terms:

Where are the boundaries of your body? Where are your population centers? Your urban renewal areas? Your deserts? Your rivers? Your mountain ranges? Cliffs? Caves? Jungles? Where are your uncharted lands? Your frontiers? If someone were to explore these uncharted lands, what might they find? Write an imaginary journey of their discoveries.

What are the chief products of your body (metaphorical as well as physical)? Natural resources? Materials for production? Energy centers? Power plants? Recreation areas? Parks? What do you most like to show to tourists? What do you imagine they would like the least? like the best?

Where are your wars and conflicts being fought? Where are your tension spots? How does someone get inside you? Who do you prohibit from entering or leaving? Is a passport needed? What are the requirements? Are there border relations? What percent of your national budget would you spend on improving these?

These don't have to be given to the students all at once, of course. You may choose to suggest two or three questions at a time over a period of several weeks. Some students will want to be assured that the material is kept confidential, which you certainly should honor.

Begin this "lesson" with a few remarks about U.S. or world geography. There are plenty of cues for you in the questions above. As you talk about geography, political boundaries, tensions and the like, lead into this activity by offering a start such as:

Now let's consider our own bodies in this geographic sense. For example, when I think of my "international" area of tension I think of my neck and shoulder muscles. At night these tensions are especially noticeable. Is that kind of like my own little "Middle East" ?

We learned this exercise from Gerald Weinstein.

A healthy person identifies with his body and feels the closeness of his ties to nature.

Alexander Lowen

The Betrayal of the Body

75

sensory awareness

Social and formal education stress the cognitive and motor functions of the organism without regard for sensory development. We teach them non-sense.

Bernard Gunther

Sense Relaxation

Owing to a lack of regard for sensory development, the people we teach are often out of touch with themselves and each other. As we teach children to "keep their hands to themselves," we soon find that they are out of contact with reality and one another. The sensory awareness method (developed by Charlotte Selver and popularized by Bernard Gunther) is a method of helping people to reclaim their ability to feel (literally) and to once again, "come to their senses."

We have collected a series of sensory awareness exercises that you can use in your classroom. As you do them, take your time—don't rush through them. When people have completed one or several exercises, allow them an opportunity to discuss what they have experienced.

1. Close your eyes and become aware of how your head feels. Bend your fingers at the joints and tap all over the top of your head. Tap the back, the sides, and the forehead. Put your hands down and experience how your head and hands feel.
2. Close your eyes and experience how your face feels. Keeping your eyes closed, begin slapping your forehead with your fingers. Both hands and fingers should be held loosely and hit the face simultaneously. Now move to the jaw, the cheeks, the lips, and the chin. Go over the nose and gently over the eyelids. Stop, lower your hands, and experience what you feel now. This slapping can be done on any or all sections of the body. You can do it to yourself or with a partner.
3. Pick a partner the same height as you. Mentally divide his body in half—right side and left side. Concentrating only on the left side, tap all over your partner's head and then slap his shoulders and left arm, back, stomach, buttocks, left leg, and foot. The person being tapped keeps his eyes closed. When this is completed, both you and your partner should stand with eyes closed and experience your own bodies. After a minute or two you should share how

you experience the difference between your right and left sides. After you have reported, the procedure should be repeated on the right side so you will feel balanced again.

4. For the entire class period use your left hand (if left-handed, use your right). Do everything you can with your weaker side. Become aware of how you feel doing this. What do you experience? Are you able to be patient with yourself? How do you experience yourself at the end of the class?

5. Pick a partner. Sit facing him. Take both of your partner's hands in both of yours. Close your eyes. Feel the contact where your hands stop and his start. Keeping your eyes closed and without *verbal* interaction, have a conversation with your hands. Allow yourself to be shy at first, then be bold. Test your partner's strength and express yours. Now have an argument. Make up. Be gentle with each other. Now express your playfulness. Now create a dance together. Let the dance subside. Say goodbye. Withdraw contact. Experience how you feel now. Open your eyes and look at your partner. Now discuss your experience with him.

6. Inhale through your nose for the count of eight. As you breath in, let your stomach come out. Then exhale through your mouth for the count of eight, letting your stomach come in. Repeat this fifteen times. This is a good exercise at the beginning of a class when all the students' energies seem to be scattered. We have also found it useful as a way to relax students before they take a test.

7. Everyone stand or sit in a circle, all facing one direction so that you are each directly behind another person. Reach out to the person in front of you and massage his neck and shoulders (3 minutes). Now turn around and do the same thing to the person who is behind you (3 minutes). This way, everyone is both simultaneously giving and receiving a massage.

8. The entire class starts to walk around. Shake both hands of each person you meet. Then shake the elbows of each person you meet. Now shake each others' shoulders. Continue on with legs, hips, heads, and noses. Afterward, stop, close your eyes, and become aware of how you feel.

There are nearly a hundred more Sensory Awareness Exercises in Bernard Gunther's two books, *Sense Relaxation* (New York, Collier Books, 1968) and *What To Do till the Messiah Comes* (New York, Collier Books, 1971). We highly recommend them both. They are both beautiful visual experiences as well as rich sources of usable material. Also see *Sensory Awareness: The Rediscovery of Experiencing* by Charles V. W. Brooks (New York: Viking Press, 1974).

> *Education ideally is an active, interested exploration: skill, learning, knowing, doing. Too much of formal education is dulling, memorization, passive compartmentalization, indoctrination.*
>
> Bernard Gunther
> *Sense Relaxation*

76

moving
with mindfulness

Mindfulness is a Buddhist term meaning "the attitude of full awareness." To perform an act with awareness qualitatively changes the experience of the act. The exercises that follow are designed to help students become more aware of how they experience themselves when they center their attention on their bodies rather than on their external environment. Ask them to try each of the "experiments" in two ways. The first time they are to perform as they normally do; the second time they are to concentrate on their bodily experience as they do it. They can pretend that there are two parts to themselves during the exercise. The first part is the person doing the exercise; the second part is the observer. Allow two or three minutes for each experiment. Follow the experiments with a discussion of what the students experienced.

1. Lift your right arm and bring it back down again several times. Now lift your arm again several times, only this time pay attention to how you will your arm to move; experience the movement, and be aware of how you stop. If you feel like resisting my invitation to move your arm, experience what resisting is like. Discuss what you experienced.

2. Go over to somebody and shake hands with him in your usual polite way, saying "Hello. How are you?" Be aware of what that feels like. Now go to the same person and shake hands again, but this time be aware of the experience of making contact with another living being. Be aware of what it's like to be fully present with and for another person. Discuss the difference.

3. Walk around the room as if you are in a hurry to get somewhere, as if the destination is what is important. After doing this for a while, walk around the room with your awareness on the process of walking rather than on any destination. Feel how your body moves, how your feet contact the floor (do this exercise without shoes if possible), how your joints move, how your muscles contract and release, and how your breathing feels. Discuss the difference.

4. Crawl around the room on your hands and knees. Do this first in a carefree way and then in a mindful way—with awareness.

5. (Put on some music for the students to move to. The music should be joyful and rhythmic.) Move in whatever stylized ways you usually dance to music. After a few minutes, close your eyes and move to the music with an

awareness of how your body feels as you move. Really take the time to see how your body "wants" to move rather than just doing some step you have learned. After the music is over, discuss what happened.

There is no form of mental existence independent of a person's physical existence. To think otherwise is an illusion.

Alexander Lowen
Depression and the Body

77

spontaneous movement

This is an exercise drawn from the practice of psychosynthesis. The basic technique is as follows: A person asks himself a question and then waits to see what movement emerges in his body. This can be done with eyes open or closed. Our experience is that it is usually more effective with eyes closed, but this doesn't hold true for everybody.

After a period of movement, which may be gross or subtle, shortlived or prolonged, singular in focus or a series of movements, the student is directed to write down his experience so that he will not lose the quality of this symbolic expression from his deeper self. Once he has recorded his impressions, he is instructed to attempt to interpret the meaning of the movement or movements.

We have found this exercise to be especially effective with students in the eighth grade and above. Some questions that you may wish to suggest for this exercise are:

> What aspect of my life do I need to give attention to now?
> What is the next step in my personal growth?
> What obstacles do I face in taking that next step?
> What quality or qualities do I need to develop to overcome these obstacles?
> How can I better relate to people?
> What do I really want to do now?

These questions are only possibilities. Actually any question could be asked. The whole point is that there is a part of us—our higher self, our inner wisdom—which knows the answer to almost any question we have that involves our being and becoming in the world. This self speaks to us in symbolic fashion, such as in dreams, intuitive flashes, strains of music that run through our minds for seemingly no reason, etc. Body movement is one of these forms of symbolic expression—thus the importance of dance in traditional religions. If we learn to ask ourselves meaningful questions and are truly receptive to the answers we are given, spontaneous movement can be very useful in our quest for self-knowledge.

Using the same questions, you might also ask the students to simply close their eyes, ask themselves a question, and wait for an image or symbol to form in their mind.

Ask them to draw this image in their journal and then attempt to interpret its meaning. Then they may discuss their experiences in the group.

We learned these two exercises from Martha Crampton.

You cannot teach a man anything. You can only help him discover it within himself.

Galileo

"And after difficult soul-searching travail through Zen, I Ching
divination, brown rice, pot, meditation, and a lengthy pilgrimmage
to India, you will eventually find happiness with
Norman Vincent Peale."

Saturday Review, December 19, 1970

five
where am I going?

We are great believers in goal-setting, intentionality, and the use of the will. Our rules for responsible self-growth are:

1. **Become aware of yourself.**
   Ultimately, this includes not just being aware of your physical and mental self, but your emotions as well—even aware of your unconscious drives and motivations. Ask yourself the question, "What am I doing? Is it getting me what I want? If not, what is it getting me?"

2. **Take responsibility for your situation.**
   This means that you must be willing to accept responsibility for the results of your behavior. In other words, if you are not getting what you want, it is probably your fault, and only through your action (i.e., by experimenting with different behaviors) are you likely to bring about different results.

3. **Look at the possible alternatives.**
   What other choices of behavior are open to you? What tentative models are more consistent with your values? What are the likely consequences of being more like this or that or of trying on a certain new behavior? What is the best thing that could happen? What is the worst thing that could happen?

4. **Choose among the alternatives.**
   What general things do you really *want* to work on? What qualities do you *want* to manifest in your life? What specific behaviors do you want to try out for the next week, month, etc.? (Note the use of the word *want* rather than *should*. True personal growth happens when a person follows his immediate striving for a greater ideal, *not* when he feels driven by "shoulds.") Decide on a behavior to try out.

5. **Affirm your decision.**
   Using the power of fantasy and belief, imagine yourself manifesting this new behavior in a variety of situations. Place a poster or a motto

reinforcing your chosen quality or behavior in a permanent place where you will see it a lot (for example, on the refrigerator, next to the bathroom mirror, over your desk, etc.). Develop and meditate upon a seed thought which reinforces your new attitude or behavior. (Examples of seed thoughts are "I can become whatever I want to." "I don't have to please everyone all the time." "I can stand up for what I believe in rather than going along with the crowd.")

6. **Develop a plan of action.**
Map out in detail the specific steps of your plan in the order you will need to take them.

7. **Act! Now!**
At some point you must actually take the risk of "trying on" the new behavior.

8. **Evaluate the outcome.**
Evaluate the results of your attempts. What happened? How did you feel during and afterward? Were the results worth the risk? If you are willing to add this new behavior or attitude to your repertoire, you have become expanded—there is a greater range of existence available to you. You have grown.[1]

The activities in this section are designed to help students get started on their journeys of self-growth. From you they will need occasional insights, a little push up a particularly difficult hill, but mostly they will need your empathic understanding and support.

We believe that this journey can be one of life's most exciting and important. The quest for self-actualization can lead our students away from the lives of alienation and anomie that can end in violence, drug abuse, sexual confusion, rebellion and apathy, and toward creative lives of commitment and growth. You can be an important part of this process simply by being willing to encourage students to be open and caring toward themselves and one another.

---

[1] For two different and more detailed versions of this model see *The Act of Will,* by Roberto Assagioli (New York: Viking Press, 1973) and "The Trumpet: An Introduction to Humanistic Education," by Gerald Weinstein. The latter appeared as an article in the November-December 1971 issue of *Theory into Practice.* A copy of the article can be obtained from the Center for Humanistic Education, University of Massachusetts, Amherst, Massachusetts 01002.

78

twenty-one questions

Hand out a sheet to each of your students with the following questions on it. Ask them to write the answers to any or all questions in whatever order they wish. When they have finished, have them discuss their answers in small groups, make "I learned. . ." statements, or discuss how the assignment made them feel. The students may want to record their responses in their journals.

1. What would you like to do, have, accomplish?
2. What do you wish would happen?
3. What would you like to do better?
4. What do you wish you had more time for? More money for?
5. What more would you like to get out of life?
6. What are your unfulfilled ambitions?
7. What angered you recently?
8. What made you tense, anxious?
9. What have you complained about?
10. What misunderstandings did you have?
11. With whom would you like to get along better?
12. What changes for the worse or better do you sense in the attitudes of others?
13. What would you like to get others to do?
14. What changes will you have to introduce?
15. What takes too long?
16. What are you wasting?
17. What is too complicated?
18. What "bottlenecks" or blocks exist in your life?
19. In what ways are you inefficient?
20. What wears you out?
21. What would you like to organize better?

This is also a good time to introduce goal-setting to your students as a technique for gaining control over their lives and achieving at least one of the things mentioned above.

Suggested by Doris Shallcross

First say to yourself what you would be; and then do what you have to do.

Epictetus
Discourses

Photo by Ginny Duff

79

FOUR DRAWINGS

Supply each student with a box of crayons and a large sheet of newsprint (if not available, use four sheets of 8½ × 11 in. paper instead). Ask the students to divide the paper into four equal sections. Tell them that they are going to draw four pictures depicting the symbolic answers to four questions you are going to have them ask themselves.

Ask them to close their eyes. You may also wish to help them to become more relaxed by doing a deep-breathing exercise such as found in Exercise 74(6) or by simply taking a minute to stretch out any tensions they may feel in their bodies. After they have had a minute or two to relax their bodies, ask them to let go of any emotions they may be feeling at the moment. Finally, ask them to quiet all the chatter of their minds so that they can become receptive to messages from their intuitive self, their true center. Tell them to imagine a blank movie screen in the middle of the forehead just above the nose. Tell them that you are going to give them a question to ask themselves, and that they should let an image be projected onto their movie screen that will represent or symbolize the answer. As soon as they have seen the image (no matter what the image is, or how unrelated it may at first seem), they are to draw it in the upper left-hand section of their papers. The later drawings will go in the remaining sections. Have them number each picture in order.

The four questions are:

1. Where am I?
2. Where am I going?
3. What obstacles will I face?
4. What inner quality will I need to develop to overcome these obstacles?

Allow about eight to ten minutes for each question and drawing. After they have completed all four drawings, ask them to share them in groups of three or four.

As you might have guessed, this exercise works best with high school age and older.

We learned this exercise from Martha Crampton and George Brown.

You alone know what you are, by the light of your innermost nature. Therefore teach me now, and hold back no word in the telling.

The Bhagavad-Gita

I want to be king because
I like to boss people.
Bob

I'd like to be a Mother
so I can drink tea.
Karen

I'd like to be an artist because
people throw flowers at your feet.
Wendy

I would like to be a puppy
because people like to hold me.
Patricia

Wishes From the Second Grade

I'd like to be a vampire
so I can rest in the morning,
stay up late in the night.
Jonathan

coffin

I would like to be a tiger
because I can pounce on people.
Robert

80

wishing

Dreams and wishes range from the simple to the fantastic. A child may simply desire a new toy or he may imagine himself walking on the moon. He can easily imagine himself to be anything or anyone he chooses. Although wishes may often seem impossible and farfetched, they are very often expressions of real needs—such as the common need to be accepted by one's peers. Once wishes are expressed and recognized as normal, they can be used as a motivating force behind action. With the use of goal-setting a child can begin to realize that, with action, some wishes may be attained.

Genies and magic fairies often grant people three wishes. Ask the children to imagine that they have three wishes. What would they be? Ask them to imagine that they had three wishes for someone else whom they liked very much. What would they wish for that person?

If they could relive the previous day, what would they wish to have been different? To have been the same?

Ask them:

Did you ever wish to be someone else? Who? Why? Do you think someone might wish to be you? Why would he want to be you?

Did you ever have a wish come true? Tell about it. Is there anything you can do, besides just wishing, to help get your wish?

> *"There's no use trying," she said, "one can't believe impossible things."*
> *"I daresay you haven't had much practice," said the Queen. "When I was your age, I always did it for half-an-hour a day. Why sometimes I've believed as many as six impossible things before breakfast."*
>
> Lewis Carroll
> *Alice in Wonderland*

81

happy package

Have the class sit in a circle. Ask the students to pretend that they can have a package any size or shape they want. Inside this imaginary box they are to place whatever it is in the whole wide world that would make them happy. Ask the students to share with the rest of the group what would be in the box and why it would make them happy.

Ask the students to share with the class things they have brought from home which make them happy.

Ask the students to leave the group, go find an object in the class that makes them happy, and return to the group and share the object.

Ask the students to share with the group a happy incident that happened to them in the past week.

Ask the students to tell the class about a person who makes them happy.

Ask the students to describe how it feels to be happy. Where do they feel it? How do they know?

Ask the students to complete the sentence: "Happiness is. . . ."

The first duty to children is to make them happy.

Sir Thomas Fowell Buxton

82

I want to be

Ask the students to list at least five people whom they admire very much. They may use names of any person whether historical, fictional, living, or dead. Ask them to write a brief essay or give a brief discussion about the person they have chosen. What qualities does that person possess? Why is he or she to be admired?

Then ask the students to compare themselves to the person they have chosen to emulate. Ask them what they would have to do to become like that person. What changes would they have to make? How could they go about making them?

Help the students set personal goals for achieving these desired changes. Ask them to share their goals with the class. Have them set deadlines for the completion of their goals. Ask them to report on their goals when the deadline arrives.

> **When I Grow Up**
> *When I grow up I*
> *Want to be me, me, me.*
> *Like my mother—she is she.*
> *And my father—he is he.*
> *So when I grow up*
> *I'm going to be me, me, me.*
>
> Jocelyn Shorin

83
MAKING YOUR WANTS KNOWN

Implicit in every question, statement of resentment, hostile comment, etc., is a demand or a "want" on the speaker's part. For example, if a student reacts to a statement of another pupil by saying something like, "Oh, that's stupid!" he really is trying to communicate, "I want. . ." or "I demand. . ." His want or demand is veiled by his hostile remark; consequently listeners can't be sure exactly what it is that he wants. How much clearer it would be if he simply stated instead, "I want to be heard on this issue" or "I demand that we vote" or whatever it is he really wants.

Some teachers will cringe at the thought of encouraging students to state their demands. Our experience, however, leads us to believe that after the initial shock to teachers and students and some experimenting with the concept, a class will settle down to a very reasonable use of this communication tool—and many wants and demands are met simply because they are clearly known to the listeners.

Begin the exercise by asking the students:

> What would make this class better for you? If you could make the people in this group do something to make the class better for you, what would you demand we do? Begin your demand or want with: "I want this class to. . ."

This exercise helps pupils realize that they do have a right to make demands on people, just as those people have a right to refuse meeting demands. At a later stage you may wnat to expand the exercise to include making demands or wants on the teacher— this usually proves to be a good feedback mechanism—and on specific students in the class. When making demands, children should face the person, say his name, and then make his want known. For instance, "Gerald, I want you to stop pulling my hair during recess" or "Martha, I want you to make less noise when I am trying to read." Some typical responses that have been generated by this exercise are:

> I demand that Nina and Lucy quit bugging me about things I bring to school.
> I want the members of this class to listen to me when I am talking.

I want the students here to share their food with me when I forget my lunch money.

This activity stems from Gestalt therapy theory.

The aim of Gestalt therapy is to develop more "intelligent" behavior; that is, to enable the individual to act on the basis of all possible information and to apprehend not only the relevant factors in the external field but also relevant information from within. The individual is directed to pay attention at any given moment to what he is feeling, what he wants, and what he is doing. The goal of such direction is non-interrupted awareness.

Elaine Kepner and Lois Brien

84

if I were
God of the universe

This activity is a projective goal-setting experience that serves as a value clarification exercise.

Ask students to imagine themselves as all-power, all-knowing gods of the universe. Then ask them to complete the following sentence: "If I were God of the Universe, I would..."

accept	stop
give up	project
respect	shut out
understand	fight
continue	remember
forget	value
change	espouse
replace	create

After each student has generated completions to these phrases, time should be given to share these completions in the class or in small groups. Students should be asked to rank-order their lists from the most important, or that which they would do first, to the least important, or that which they would do last.

We learned this exercise from Joel Goodman.

A small child was drawing a picture and his teacher said, "That's an interesting picture. Tell me about it."
"It's a picture of God."
"Well nobody knows what God looks like."
"They will when I get done."

85

the ideal model

Many of our behaviors seem to stem from models which we have incorporated sometimes consciously, but more often than not, unconsciously. These models are generally not voluntarily chosen and tend to be derived from social conditioning. They often lack the self-actualizing value of models chosen consciously.

There are two parts to this exercise. The first is designed to help students clarify and articulate the various and conflicting models that determine their behavior at the present time. This prepares the ground for use of the "ideal model" technique in which visualization is used to consciously choose and begin to actualize a model of what we wish to become. Give the following instructions:

A. *Recognizing False Models*
   We all have images of ourselves as being less adequate in certain ways than we really are. Consider some of the ways in which you *underrate* yourself (i.e., putting yourself down, judging yourself, acting as if you are not the kind of person who does this or that easily, etc.). First think about it, writing down ideas that come to you. Then close your eyes and let images or pictures come into your mind which are related to the ways in which you underrate yourself. Study these images for a few minutes, learning as much as you can about them, noting the feelings they arouse in you, and reflecting on their meaning to your life. Write down any insights you have in your journal. (10 to 15 minutes.)

   Using the same thought and visualization procedure as above, explore some of the models you have which are based on the way *you would like to appear to others* (i.e., cool, romantic, carefree, tough guy, good girl, etc.) or the ways you imagine other people would want you to be. There are probably different models involved for the different relationships in your life (e.g., with a boyfriend or girlfriend, with parents, with teachers, with various groups of friends, etc.). Consider these relationships and how you try to appear as contrasted with the way you really are. Become aware of your feelings about each of these roles you play and whether the models they are based on help or hinder your own development. Be specific in trying to articulate and label the models involved. Ask yourself what underlying assumptions you are making in each situation about what behavior is "desirable" in relation to the impression you are trying to create. Remember to use the imagining techniques as well as conscious thought on working on this question. Write down any insights you have in your journal. (10 to 15 minutes.)

> *In the coming world they will not ask me: "Why were you not Moses?"—they will ask me: "Why were you not Zusaya?"*
>
> Maurice S. Friedman
>
> *Martin Buber: The Life and Dialogue*

B. *Disidentifying from the False Models*

Imagine and feel what it would be like to let go of all of these false and imposed models of yourself. Realize that they are roles you play or that others would like you to play, but that they do not necessarily define the limits of your existence. You can play these roles if you wish to do so, but you are not locked into them and you can change them if you decide to. Close your eyes and meditate upon the concept of disidentification. (5 minutes.)

> *If a man does not keep pace with his companions, perhaps it is because he hears a different drummer. Let him step to the music which he hears, however measured or far away.*
>
> Henry David Thoreau

C. *Choosing an Ideal Model*

There are different types of "ideal models," some of a general nature which represent a fully integrated personality, and others of a more specific kind. The most practical type of ideal model to work with in the beginning is one that represents a particular quality or set of interrelated qualities (patience and tolerance or positivity, action and perseverance, serenity) you would like to develop within yourself at this time. These "qualities" can be an underdeveloped *psychological function,* such as expressing a certain feeling; or an *attitude,* such as love or calmness; an *ability,* such as learning to play a musical instrument; or a *pattern of action,* such as taking a stand for what you believe in. The ideal model must be realistic; it is a vision or a goal to inspire or magnetically "attract" us, but it must represent an attainable next step in our development. If the model feels *too idealistic,* redefine it until it feels more plausible.

Proceed as you did before, using both rational thought and the imagery technique to choose an ideal model for this point in your development. Take some time to do this. Reflect on what you would like to become and what qualities would help you to accomplish this. See if you can let your thoughts and images come from a place deep within you which is your true essential self. Write down your insights and conclusions. (10 to 15 minutes.)

D. *Identifying with the Ideal Model: The "As-If" Technique*

The power of creative imagination can be used to help translate an image or goal into *the concrete reality of everyday life.*

Having chosen an ideal model, visualize and imagine yourself in various situations in your real life acting *as if* you already possessed the quality, attitude, or ability you have chosen to develop. See yourself actually manifesting the *thoughts, feelings,* and *actions* that correspond to it. Practice in imagination your new attitude, using a variety of situations with different people and different circumstances. As you visualize this new image of yourself carrying out a specific new behavior, this is useful preparation for attempting to express these new attitudes in your real life. When you are visualizing yourself as having taken this next step, perceive your eyes, your expression, your posture, your gestures, your voice, and your words as all embodying whatever that step represents. *Feel* what it is like to think and act in this way. If any changes in your ideal model suggest themselves as you do this, feel free to make whatever corrections or refinements seem desirable. The ideal model is not intended to be static, rigid, and confining. It is flexible, dynamic, and capable of evolving in accordance with our own development and is the basis of the internal and external feedback we receive through experience in the world and inner prompting. (10 to 15 minutes.)

> *All that we are is the result of what we have thought.*
>
> Buddha

This can be a very powerful exercise. We usually devote an entire class period to it. It can be followed by a writing assignment, or as a class discussion. This exercise works best with high school age and older.

This exercise was developed by Martha Crampton. It is one of many exercises used in rapidly expanding approach to human growth called "psychosynthesis." For information on literature and workshops on psychosynthesis, write The Canadian Institute for Psychosynthesis, 3496 Marlowe Avenue, Montreal, Quebec, Canada; The Psychosynthesis Institute, 576 Everett Street, Palo Alto, California 94301; The Psychosynthesis Research Foundation, Room 1902, 40 East 49th Street, New York, New York 10017.

> *You cannot teach a man anything.*
> *You can only help him discover it within himself.*
>
> Galileo

UPI Photo

86

the goalpost

Decorate the bulletin board in the form of a football goalpost. Each day allow time for the students who would like to set a goal to record them on 3 x 5 index cards and post them on the bulletin board below the crossbar of the goalpost. If time permits, you may wish to have the class cut the index cards into the shape of footballs.

On the following day, ask all those who completed their goals to move their index card above the crossbar and to share their goal and how they completed it with the class. This provides the goal-achievers with the attention of their peer group as a reinforcement to their action.

Those who did not complete their goals are not allowed to share with the class their goals and the reasons for not accomplishing them. (If they did this, they would be receiving the same reinforcement of peer attention as those who had completed theirs. The class would also be reinforcing their behavior of rationalizing away their failure to take responsibility for achieving goals.)

This is a powerfully important exercise in that it makes explicit accomplishments that are often overlooked. It also helps students to focus on the development of the will. Another positive by-product is often improved home relationships. For example, one third-grade girl began to set goals like clearing the table without being asked, helping to do the dishes, taking out the garbage, cleaning her room, etc. A week later her amazed mother called her teacher and wanted to know what had happened.

We have found the following goal-setting guidelines very helpful in determining the criteria for effective goal-setting. (see Exercise 86a.)

> *"Cheshire-Puss," she began, rather timidly. . ."Would you tell me, please, which way I ought to go from here?"*
> *"That depends a good deal on where you want to get to," said the cat.*
> *"I don't much care where. . .", said Alice.*
> *"Then it doesn't matter which way you go," said the cat.*
>
> Lewis Carroll
> *Alice in Wonderland*

86a
guidelines for goal-setting

Once a person has decided where he is, who he is, and where he wants to go, he has identified what success means to him. Now he needs to learn how to establish goals to carry him along the road to success. To set effective goals, it is important that one observe the following guidelines. A goal must be:

1. *Conceivable*
   You must be able to conceptualize the goal so that it is understandable and then be able to identify clearly what the first step or two would be.

2. *Believable*
   In addition to being consistent with your personal value system, you must believe you can reach the goal. This goes back to the need to have a positive, affirmative feeling about one's self. Bear in mind that few people can believe a goal that they have never seen achieved by someone else. This has serious implications for goal-setting in culturally deprived areas.

3. *Achievable*
   The goals you set must be accomplishable with your given strengths and abilities. For example, if you were a rather obese 45-year-old, it would be foolish for you to set the goal of running the four-minute mile in the next six months—that simply would not be achievable.

4. *Controllable*
   If your goal includes the involvement of anyone else, you should first obtain the permission of the other person or persons to be involved; or the goal may be stated as an invitation. For example, if your goal were to take your girlfriend to a movie on Saturday night, the goal would not be acceptable as stated because it involves the possibility that she might turn you down. However, if you said your goal was merely to invite your girlfriend to the movie, it would be acceptable.

5. *Measurable*
   Your goal must be stated so that it is measurable in time and quantity.
   For example, suppose your goal were to work on your term paper this week. You would specify your goal by saying, "I am going to write *twenty pages* by 3:00 P.M. next Monday." That way, the goal can be measured; and when Monday comes, you know whether or not you have achieved it.

6. *Desirable*

Your goal should be something you really want to do. Whatever your ambition, it should be one that you want to fulfill, rather than something you feel you should do. We are well aware that there are many things in life a person has to do, but if he is to be highly motivated, he must commit a substantial percentage of his time to doing things he wants to do. In other words, there should be a balance in life, but the "want" factor is vital to changing style of being and living.

7. *Stated with No Alternative*

You should set one goal at a time. Our research has shown that a person who says he wants to do one thing or another—giving himself an alternative—seldom gets beyond the "or." He does neither. This does not imply inflexibility. Flexibility in action implies an ability to be able to make a judgment that some action you are involved in is either inappropriate, unnecessary, or the result of a bad decision. Even though you may set out for one goal, you can stop at any time and drop it for a new one. But when you change, you again state your goal without an alternative.

8. *Growth-Facilitating*

Your goal should never be destructive to yourself, to others, or to society. A student recently set a goal to break off fourteen car antennas before 9:00 A.M. the next day. The goal was certainly believable, achievable, measurable, and so forth. Obviously such a goal cannot be supported. If a student is seeking potentially destructive goals, an effort to encourage him to consider a different goal should be made.

These guidelines have been adapted from
Choose Success: How to Set and Achieve All Your Goals,
by Dr. Billy B. Sharp with Claire Cox
(New York: Hawthorn Books, 1970).

Who Am I

In this oversized world?

One little spec.

Not a leader

Not a follower

Just a nobody.

Does fate have something planned for me???

Or will I die within the next hour?

Or year?

Or fifty years?

Will I ever be a someone?

Probably not.

But wait!

I could be a someone.

Yes, I someone to a noone who is someone to me!

I may not be anything big to the world,

But I might be, to one small spec of that world.

by Elaine Beaulieu

87

FIVE YEARS AHEAD: RESUME

FIVE YEARS AHEAD

After each student has engaged in the strength bombardment exercise (see Exercise 40), ask him to fantasize for himself or for another what kind of person he would be and what he would be doing five years from now if he fully developed and used all the strengths he identified in himself. Then ask him to write in his journal a description of that person (five years from now, with his strengths fully developed) and what his life is like.

We learned this exercise from Billy Sharp.

RESUMÉ

Explain to the students the function of a resumé in job seeking. If you have a copy of a resumé available, share it with your students. Brainstorm with the students some possible categories (scholastic achievements, hobbies, athletic successes, skills they have attained, jobs they have held, etc.) they could use in creating a resumé for themselves. Then ask them to imagine a job they would like to hold. Have them share their choices with the class. Ask them to list the past accomplishments, personal strengths, and skills they have that they would "sell" to their prospective employer or interviewer in order to secure the job. Have them create a resumé and role-play such an interview.

We received the idea for this exercise from Audrey Peterson.

> The idea expressed in the Biblical "love thy neighbor as thyself!" implies that respect for one's own integrity and uniqueness, love for and understanding of one's own self, cannot be separated from respect and love and understanding for another individual. The love for my own self is inseparably connected with love for any other being.
>
> Erich Fromm
> *The Art of Loving*

88

the six o'clock news

Have kids write a TV news report beginning with a dateline and telling something that the writer might do as of some future date. The newscast should elaborate on the major events of the person's life. The six o'clock news becomes a kind of "hoped-for" autobiography.

Example:

June 4, 1984

A TV-8 exclusive!

Yesterday a young American woman named Patricia Riggs was elected President of Cuba. Miss Riggs is the first American citizen to be elected president of another nation and also the first non-Cuban to be elected to a major office in that Caribbean country. Miss Riggs' climb from obscurity in Chicago to prominence in world politics is almost unbelievable. Her early professional career was teaching.

> *Goodnight, Chet.*
> *Goodnight, David.*
>
> Chet Huntley and David Brinkley

six

the language
of self

The field of general semantics has made an important contribution to the humanistic movement. Some teachers have been particularly skilled in applying general semantics principles to the classroom situation in order to build an affective environment and create intrapersonal awareness.[1]

It is certainly well known that our language effects our thinking. For example, we often say somebody "is" something. Our thinking is thereby conditioned to accept the notion that whatever that quality "is," it sure enough resides in the person! In truth however, to say that somebody "is" something only means that *the speaker attributes* that quality to the person. Quite a difference! Several other "tools for improving thinking" are included in Keyes's *How to Develop Your Thinking Ability.*[2]

This section, "The Language of Self," is composed primarily of activities that have a general semantics base. Students usually find them quite fascinating.[3]

---

[1] Harold C. Wells, "To Get Beyond the Words. . .", *Educational Leadership,* Association for Supervision and Curriculum Development, December, 1970.

[2] Kenneth S. Keyes, Jr., *How to Develop Your Thinking Ability* (New York: McGraw-Hill), p. 147.

[3] If you or your pupils wish to pursue this field further, some excellent references are J. Samuel Bois, *The Art of Awareness* (Dubuque, Iowa: Wm. Brown Co., 1966 and Mary S. Morain, ed., *Teaching General Semantics* (San Francisco: International Society for General Semantics, 1969); also The International Society for General Semantics, 540 Powell Avenue, San Francisco, California; and Viewpoints Institute, P. O. Box 1124, Beverly Hills, California. Finally, we also recommend John P. Steven's *Awareness* (Moab, Utah: Real People Press, 1971; paperback, New York: Bantam Books, 1973). This book contains many useful exercises to use in developing awareness of how our language affects us.

IS IS WHAT WAS WAS?

Tom Hicks
Etc.

An *is* is just a *was* that was
and that is very small. . .
And *is* is *was* so soon it almost
wasn't *is* at all.
For *is* is only *is* until
it is a *was*—you see. . .
And as an *is* advances—to
remain an *is* can't be. . .
'cause if *is* is to stay an *is*
it isn't *is* because
another *is* is where it was
and *is* is then a *was*.

Toussowasket '69

Noll C. Derriksan

194

89
WORDS THAT DESCRIBE ME

Ask your students to write down three words that describe themselves. Given thoughtful attention, any three words that come to mind are appropriate. They can be descriptive of physical, emotional, mental, personality, or character traits.

When they have done that, ask them to turn the paper over and write three words they *wish* described themselves.

Now have each person take one of the three words on his second list and describe *specific* behaviors that that kind of person exhibits. For example, Charlie says, "I want to be kind." What specific behaviors do "kind" people exhibit?

They help people in distress:

> Take food to someone who is hungry
> Mow the lawn for a neighbor who is injured or ill
> Baby-sit temporarily for a working mother while she finds a replacement for a "permanent" sitter who quit

What else do "kind" people do?

They are considerate of other's feelings:

> Sally says, "I hate doing the dishes!" A kind person may respond, "Let me help you."
> Billy spills milk on the floor and Ben says, "Billy you sure are clumsy!" A kind person might retort, "No, he's not clumsy, he simply spilled his milk!"

Your class will need some help being specific enough to do any good, so give some examples on the board using words from a couple of students' lists.

When each student has completed listing specific behaviors for one of his words, ask him to use that word as a goal. Use the behaviors as some suggested ways of meeting that goal. If Charlie wants to be "kind" he can immediately start to practice some of the behaviors he has listed and can begin to look for other opportunities as well.

This exercise develops self-esteem only if people work at doing something about their goal. You can help assure this by having a five-minute session once a week in which students state their goals and give examples of something they've done to help accomplish them.

"I have hairy arms, one wart on my pinky finger, kitten scratches all over my hands, red lips and a small nose."

Lawrence Branagan and Christopher Moroney

90

I am not my description

In the previous activity, students were asked to write three words that described themselves. Many people, given such an opportunity write words that are negative in connotation. For example, one young boy wrote: "bad; I fight; dumb."

The trouble starts when we assume that labels like "bad" and "dumb" are actually us! These self-labels are repeated by us over and over until they affect our every action. Repeated internally for years, they have the cumulative effect of being terribly self-crippling.

Use the negative words that your students wrote in the previous exercise or ask them to write down two "bad" things about themselves. Pick them up and list all the items on a large sheet of paper (you'll want to save it for the next activity).

Discuss the items listed in reference to their reality (don't identify the writer). "Are you *always* 'bad'?" "Under what circumstances are you 'bad'?" Help your class through this discussion to realize that what they considered as "bad" characteristics are nothing more (or less) than labels they've applied to certain kinds of behavior that occurred in particular situations in the past. There is no point in applying those labels to their present situations and certainly not to the future.

Show them how to rewrite their "bad" words to make them more realistic, more scientific, and less damaging to themselves. This involves writing about specific behaviors, specific times, in specific situations. An illustration might be: "Yesterday I hit a boy" (rather than "I'm bad" or "I fight a lot") or "I haven't learned to multiply by 8's or 9's (rather than "I'm dumb about arithmetic."). Notice that the rewritten sentences do not imply worthlessness in the present or hopelessness for the future. Now have them rewrite their words.

As an assignment, have your students keep track for a day of every time they tell themselves they are "bad" (*or act as if* they were).

Follow this up with a class discussion.

> *Whatever one believes to be true either is true or becomes true in one's mind.*
> John C. Lilly
> *The Center of the Cyclone*

91

the tyranny of "should"

This is a follow-up to the previous activity. Use the same words, if possible.

Many of the words your students used to describe "bad" things about themselves implied that they *should* or *ought to* be this or that. For example, some kids are apt to say, "I'm ugly," or "I'm fat," or "I'm afraid." All these words imply that they should be the opposite: "I should be beautiful!"; "I ought to be thin"; or "I should be brave!" Several things are wrong here but we'll deal with only one and save another for the next activity.

Who says everybody *ought* to look like Clark Gable or Marilyn Monroe, and that anyone who looks very different from that general conception of beauty is ugly? Who says we all *should* be brave or thin? These are culturally induced values that may or may not be appropriate to specific situations. The fantastic psychological damage that has been done to most of us by our *believing* the Hollywood conception of beauty is inestimable. So it is with numerous other values that we derive from our society. Our mental health can be improved by understanding that "should" and "ought to," when applied indiscriminately to culturally induced values are, in fact, prejudicial—because we believe in advance that we *should* look or behave in certain ways, and consequently we do not view each new event as a fresh experience to feel about and react to as we naturally would, but instead spend our time anxiously concerned with "shoulds" and "oughts."

When you've discussed this idea with your class, have the students form small groups of six to eight people. Their task is to list as many examples as they can of things we *should* believe according to our culture. For example:

> It is "good" to work.
> It is "good" to own many things.
> Blondes have more fun.
> If you are a man working in an office, you "should" wear a tie.
> Everyone "ought" to be a good reader.

When the groups are done, list their contributions on the chalkboard and discuss them.

Have each individual write a page about his two "bad" things in which he tells why it is damaging to him to continue to believe that he *ought to* (whatever his "should" is).

> *This above all—to thine own self be true;*
> *And it must follow, as the night the day,*
> *Thou canst not then be false to any man.*
>
> Shakespeare

92

scientific language

There is another simple idea from the field of general semantics that you can teach your students to help them get a better perspective on the "bad" things about themselves. Use the same list of words or phrases you compiled from the previous two or three activities.

We often attribute value to something as though only two value choices existed—things are assumed to be good or bad, white or black, dirty or clean, right or wrong, etc.

Take some of the "bad" things your pupils wrote about themselves. Notice how often they *imply* a two-valued system as they say, "I am bad" as though there were only two alternatives. Point out to them that even such terribly abstract concepts as good and bad fall on a continuum—a line with "good" at one end and "bad" on the other; and that an enormous range of behaviors can be classified along the line, some "better" or "worse" than others.

Take the list of words your students gave you, pick out a couple that illustrate this point, and talk to your class about them. Draw a continuum using one of their words or phrases. Discuss various points on the continuum to show how opposites blend together as there are *degrees* of "badness" and "goodness" or whatever it is you are using as concepts.

At this point, if you've followed this sequence of three lessons, your students should realize that (1) they often label themselves as if they always were and always will be their label, (2) they often make themselves unhappy by believing they *should* be some idealized image they've learned from society, and (3) they are frequently victims of two-valued logic (things are either one thing or its opposite).

Break your class into groups of four and assign each group the task of developing a small play or skit that illustrates these ideas. They should perform both the unscientific and scientific ways of dealing with these concepts.

Every belief is a limit to be examined and transcended.

John C. Lilly
The Center of the Cyclone

I TAUGHT THEM ALL

Naomi White
Progressive Education
November 1943

I have taught in high school for ten years. During that time I have given assignments, among others, to a murderer, a pugilist, a thief and an imbecile. The murderer was a quiet little boy who sat on the front seat and regarded me with pale blue eyes; the pugilist lounged by the window and let loose at intervals in a raucous laugh that startled even the geraniums; the thief was a gay-hearted Lothario with a song on his lips; and the imbecile, a shifty-eyed little animal seeking the shadows.

The murderer awaits death in the state penitentiary; the pugilist lost an eye in a brawl in Hong Kong; the thief, by standing on tip-toe, can see the window of my room from the county jail; and the once gentle-eyed little moron beats his head against a padded wall in the state asylum.

All these pupils once sat in my room, sat and looked at me gravely across worn brown desks. I must have been a great help to those pupils. . .I taught them the rhyming scheme of the Elizabethan sonnet and how to diagram a complex sentence.

93

I CAN'T...I WON'T

Ask the students to find partners. Have them take turns saying sentences that start with the words "I can't. . ." Ask them to consider their school life, their social life, their home life, etc., as possible areas from which to draw these statements.

After about four or five minutes, ask them to go back and repeat all the sentences they have just said with one change: replacing the word *can't* with the word *won't* or *I don't want to.* Explain to them that the words "I won't" may not feel right to them the first time they say them, but that it is like going into a clothing store and trying on a coat. It may not fit you, but you won't know that until you try it on. Just because you say it, doesn't mean you are stuck with it forever. It is simply an experiment to discover how we experience ourselves differently after saying "I won't" instead of "I can't."

Ask them to repeat exactly what they said before except for the substitution of "won't" for "can't," and to take the time to be aware of how they experience saying each sentence. Again, give them about five minutes to do this.

Bring the class back together and ask them what they experienced as they did the exercise. Did they experience any difference between saying "I can't" and "I won't"? Usually responses will include such statements as:

> I felt more powerful when I said, "I won't!"
> I felt like "I can't" was a copout.
> I felt like I was more in charge with "I won't."
> When I said "I can't," it was as if there was some outside force controlling me. With "I won't" I realized that the decision to do it or not to do it was all in me.
> I sounded whiney when I said, "I can't."
> "I won't" sounded more true to me.

Ask them to consider whether their "I can't" statements are really statements of something that is impossible, or whether it is something possible that they simply refuse to do. Ask them to become aware of and to affirm their power of refusal. "I can't" implies being unable, crippled, and controlled from the outside. "I won't" affirms the responsibility for their actions. Often this reaffirmation of responsibility

even leads to the transformation of an "I can't" to an "I will."

After you have used this exercise with your class, make a habit of correcting people in class who say "I can't." Ask them to repeat whatever they have said with the words "I won't."

We learned this exercise from Judy Ohlbaum-Canfield.

It is in intentionality and will that the human being experiences his identity. "I" is the "I" of "I can." Descartes was wrong when he wrote, "I think, therefore I am," for identity does not come out of thinking as such, and certainly not out of intellectualization. Descartes' formulation leaves out exactly the variable that is most significant; it jumps from thought to identity, when what actually occurs is the intermediate variable of "I can." What happens in human experiences is "I conceive—I can—I will—I am." The "I can" and "I will" are the essential experiences of identity.

Rollo May
Love and Will

94

please...no!;...yes...no!

Recently a student introduced us to this little dialogue game, which turned out to be valuable for some of our pupils. It is not unlike some of John O. Stevens' awareness activities.

Pair up your class or group and have them decide which of them will be A and which B. Stop the process right here and ask them to examine and discuss with one another how the choice of who was A and who was B was made. "Is there a pattern in your life that is exemplified by your taking the lead and deciding which letter you would be? It is typical of you to let someone else decide such matters? If your partner had been of the opposite sex from what he or she is, would that have affected how your letter would have been chosen? Think about it!"

Now go back to your original activity. Have the A's take the part of the please-sayer; the B's each time are to respond with "No!" Keep this up, one saying "Please" and the other "No!" until the no-sayer (B) feels that the pleader has reached a deep sense of sincerity and humility in his request. Then he responds with "Yes!"

Have the partners change roles. Obviously there is no particular subject matter for the "please" request. Each player may make whatever assumptions he wishes about it, but the "thing" is not to be decided upon.

One of our students revealed that she couldn't play the part of the please-sayer. She said, "I've always got to be on top." That was an insightful and honest confrontation with herself and the class and the moment was treated in such an accepting way as to justify her trust in our understanding.

A variation of this exercise is to have the A's say "Yes!" and the B's respond with "No!" Let it develop into a lively two-word conversation using only the words "yes" and "no." Learning to say "No!" is very important—if they don't learn to say it, people may allow themselves to be walked over by other people's expectations and desires. In reality a real "yes" cannot exist without the ability to say "no." If one is not able to say "no" with a straight face and mean it, then his "yes" is no more than a conditioned reflex action.

> *Trust is the pacemaker variable in group growth. From it stem all the other significant variables of health. That is, to the extent that trust develops, people are able to communicate genuine feelings and perceptions of relevant issues to all members of the system.*
>
> Lorraine M. Gibb

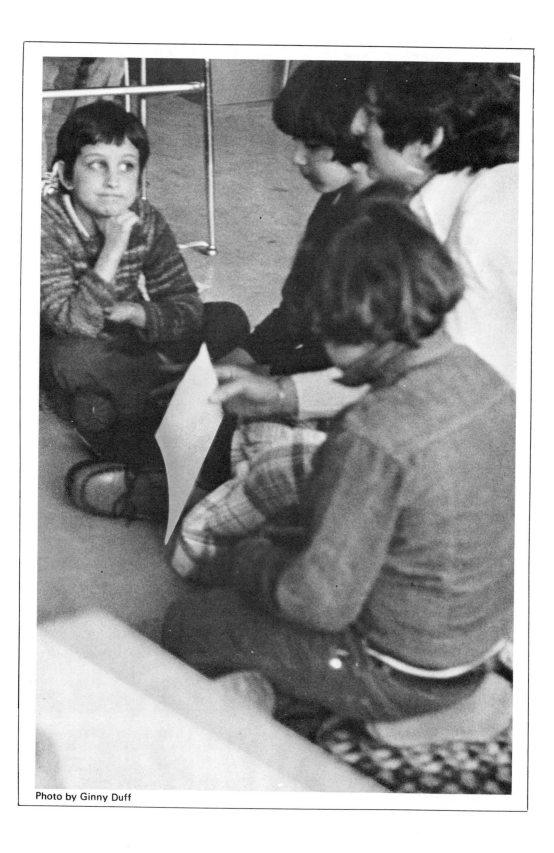

Photo by Ginny Duff

95

volunteering

An interesting and profitable exercise for many people is this simple imagination technique. As the leader, you suggest to the group that you're going to ask for a volunteer in a couple of minutes to do "something in front of the class." Pause for a considerable time and then proceed by saying something like, "I don't think you'll find it embarrassing to do, but it may take someone with quite a bit of nerve to be up here." Again pause. If someone volunteers, just ignore that person. Again proceed, "Well, I'm sure you want to know more before you volunteer, but I'd prefer not to reveal any more at this moment." Pause again.

Now smile and say you've just been putting them on—you don't really want a volunteer. Notice the reaction of relief! Have the group discuss their feelings about volunteering. How many were prepared to volunteer? Some people will resent the put-on. Deal with that but don't let it sidetrack the "to volunteer or not" issue.

When you've discussed these things for a few minutes, have everyone close their eyes and imagine two selves, one a volunteering self and the other a nonvolunteering self. Have these two imaginative characters engage in a dialogue in each participant's mind. After three or four minutes of quiet for the fantasy exercise, invite the group to share what their figures were saying.

Ask, "Which won the argument, your volunteering or nonvolunteering self? What arguments were used by the winner? Did you use these same arguments when you were considering my request for a volunteer? To what extent do you say negative things about yourself because you don't like to be the center of attraction? How is your self-concept affected by these kinds of statements?"

When you ask me how I feel, I'm the only one who can tell you! And I like that!

Kindergarten student

"I like my room the best of all my inside places because off of my closet there is a little attic room that is all mine."

Lawrence Branagan and Christopher Moroney

96

incomplete sentences

Incomplete sentences provide the student with an opportunity to get more insight into himself based on the unrehearsed quality of the answers that emerge from completing the sentences listed below with whatever pops into their head first. Incomplete sentences can be used one at a time as a basis for starting a discussion, as a cue for journal writing, or they can be used several at a time to give students a lot of data about a similar subject (such as "friends") from which they can extract a pattern about their responses.

The sentence stubs listed below are just a beginning. Using your imagination, you and other teachers, or even the kids themselves, can generate many more. Just tune into the things that your students would most naturally be concerned with. The range is quite wide.

I really get a lot of pleasure when I. . .

If I were president, the first thing I would do is. . .

My idea of a good job is. . .

The thing I like people to admire me for is. . .

Something I've never told anyone about before is. . .

I'd like my friends to. . .

If I could spend all my time at school in one course, it would be. . .

I am cool when I. . .

I am happiest when I. . .

I love to. . .

I like to hear stories about. . .

I get turned on by. . .

I like myself because. . .

I feel best when people. . .

Something I'm really good at is. . .

I'd like my parents to. . .

The one thing I most want to accomplish is. . .

I am. . .

I want to be. . .

I used to. . .

I don't like to. . .

The world would be a better place if people would. . .

The thing I'm most concerned about is. . .

I feel important when. . .

I seem to get my way when. . .

The best thing about my body is. . .

I can. . .

I want to. . .

See the next exercise for more incomplete sentences.

Photo by Kathryn Woringer

97

identity, connectedness, and power

In their book *Toward Humanistic Education: A Curriculum of Affect*, Gerald Weinstein and Mario Fantini suggest that there are three areas of concern that people seem to spend most of their time thinking about:

> *Identity* basically deals with the question "Who am I?" Various forms of this question are: Why am I a girl? Why was I born black? What do I really feel about things? How come I act the way I do? How come I'm in the dumb class? What's really important in life? What can I do to be more happy?

> *Connectedness* deals with the issue of my relationships with others in my world. Typical concerns from this area are: Who are my friends? What are my values? To whom do I owe my allegiance? How do I make new friends? What do I want from other people? What am I willing to give up of myself to get what I want from others?

> *Power* refers to the sense of control over one's own life. Typical expressions about one's concern with power are: I can do anything I set my mind to! Why should I even try; nothing ever works out the way I want it to. I don't have a chance, man; I have to do what they say. How can I get a good job with a C average?

What we've done below is to list more incomplete sentences similar to those in the previous exercise, only this time we have divided them into the three areas of identity, connectedness, and power. Most of these have been brainstormed by teachers that have been in our training workshops. A group of five teachers can usually generate over fifty sentence stubs in a period of five or six minutes. So, when you run out of these, get together with some other teachers and invent some more. It's easy—and profitable!

IDENTITY

My favorite . . . is . . .
If I could have one wish, it would be . . .
I'm happiest when I . . .
I feel the saddest when . . .
I feel most important when I . . .

One question I have about life is . . .
I get angry when . . .
A fantasy I enjoy is . . .
A thought I keep having is . . .
When I get angry I . . .

When I feel sad I. . .
When I feel scared I. . .
I get scared when. . .
Something I want but I'm afraid to ask for is. . .
I feel brave when. . .
I felt brave when. . .
I love to. . .
I see myself as. . .
Something I do well is. . .
I worry about my. . .
My greatest asset is. . .
I often think about. . .
More than anything else, I would like to. . .
If I were an adult I would. . .
If I were a little kid I would. . .

The best thing about being me is. . .
The worst thing about being me is. . .
I hate. . .
I need. . .
I wonder about. . .
I bet. . .
I feel like my mother/father when. . .
I do my best work when. . .
My body is. . .
My face is. . .
I feel uncomfortable when. . .
The thing I'm most afraid to talk about is. . .
I don't want to. . .
I am afraid to. . .
I wish I had the courage to. . .

CONNECTEDNESS

People are. . .
My friends are. . .
The thing that makes me a good friend
    is. . .
The things I look for in a friend are. . .
My parents. . .
My brother(s)/sister(s). . .
Other people make me feel. . .
Older people are. . .
Younger people are. . .
I wish people would. . .
I wish my family would. . .
I like people who. . .
I don't like people who. . .
I believe. . .
I value. . .
I make friends by. . .
My best friend. . .
My teacher. . .
I wish my teacher would. . .
The other students in this class. . .

Girls. . .
Boys. . .
People can get to me by. . .
Teasing people is. . .
When people tease me I. . .
When someone tells me they like me, I. . .
People like me because. . .
People think I am. . .
I think I am. . .
Someone I'd like to get to know better
    is. . .
Something I do for my mother is. . .
Something I do for my father is. . .
I like it when somebody says to me. . .
I wish I had told. . .
I stop myself from talking in class by
    imagining that. . .
I resent. . .for. . .
I appreciate. . .
I demand. . .
I pretend to be. . .when I'm really. . .

POWER

Something I do well is. . .

Something I'm getting better at is. . .

I can. . .

I am proud that I. . .

I get people's attention by. . .

I get my way by. . .

My greatest strength is. . .

I can help other people to. . .

I taught someone how to. . .

I need help on. . .

I'm learning to. . .

I feel big when. . .

I have the power to. . .

I was able to decide to. . .

When people try to boss me around, I. . .

I don't like people to help me with. . .

Something I can do all by myself is. . .

People can't make me. . .

I got into trouble when I. . .

I get praise from others when I. . .

The most powerful person I know is. . .

People seem to respect me when I. . .

I want to be able to. . .

I want to be strong enough to. . .

A time when I was a leader was. . .

I'm not afraid to. . .

Something that I can do now that I couldn't do last year is. . .

When I want my parents to do something, I. . .

I have difficulty dealing with. . .

People who expect a lot from me make me feel. . .

I have accomplished. . .

If I want to, I can. . .

People who agree with me make me feel. . .

Strong independent people. . .

If I were the teacher I would. . .

Photo by Janet Goto

seven
relationships
with others

> People acquire and maintain, and enrich their sense of worthwhileness only if they at least vaguely recognize the sources of what personal identity they have: their family, their friends and neighbors, their associates or fellow workers, their group ties, or their nation.[1]

This a critical idea. Self-esteem is related to the recognition that we achieve our identity through relationships with other people. We think immediately of John Donne's statement that "No man is an island." The quest for self-actualization has never meant "self without others." There *is* no self without others, although there may be periods of withdrawal. In the final analysis we find our being with others and must return to them to serve. This is well illustrated in Zen philosophy by the tenth and final Ox-herding Picture (portraying the journey to enlightenment), which shows enlightened man "entering the market place with helping hands."[2]

In this section we pay particular attention to family and friends. It is these two groups that are especially influential to our developing selves. Most of the exercises in this book imply the quality of *relationship.* It is a truism that self-love precedes love of others. Hence, we have concentrated on *self*-awareness, *self*-identity, and *self*-esteem, knowing that these are prerequisites to loving others. It seems quite appropriate then that our final section deals with "relationships with others."

---

[1] Hadley Cantril, "A Fresh Look at the Human Design", in *Challenges of Humanistic Psychology,* by James F. T. Bugental (New York: McGraw-Hill, 1967).

[2] Phillip Kapleau, *The Three Pillars of Zen* (Boston: Beacon Press, 1965).

"My mother and father are very kind. I like them very much."

Lawrence Branagan and Christopher Moroney

98

THE FAMILY

The dynamics and relationships of the family are constant sources of confusion for children. Here are several exercises designed to help children explore and accept their feelings about their families.

Ask the students to describe their feelings about their older and younger sisters and brothers. Recount some of your own experiences to the children first.

Ask the students who have brothers or sisters to write an essay describing their relationship(s) with them. The students who are only children may write on the topic: "Why I would like to have a brother or sister." It is always an enlightening experience to have the children compare the two types of papers.

Have students write about a situation in which the members of their families showed kindness and understanding toward one another.

Give them the opportunity to talk or write about what it would be like to be an orphan.

Ask each child to write a composition describing how each member of his family, including himself, is unique and different. How do these differences contribute to a stronger family?

Using the voting technique described in Exercise 51, ask the students the following questions:

> How many of you like one parent more than the other?
> How many of you have no father living at home?
> How many of you have ever wished that one of your family would go away and stay away?
> How many of you have ever wished that you were dead?
> How many of you wish you were the father or mother?
> How many of you have ever disliked your mother, if only for a moment?
> How many of you have ever disliked your father, if only for a moment?
> Did you notice how many other people had the same feelings as you? It is quite

normal to sometimes hate the people you love. It is also quite normal not to love everybody the same.

A nightmare is the child's way of telling in pictures what he fears to tell in words. It is better for children to express jealousy and anger in words rather than in a nightmare.

Haim G. Ginott
Between Parent and Child

99

family tree

The purpose of this activity is to help each student understand and appreciate some of his heritage.

Explain to the children what a family tree is. To illustrate, you might draw your own on the chalkboard. For homework, have the children ask their parents for the necessary data about their relatives to enable them to complete their family trees.

In class, help them translate the data they have gathered into a family tree. To heighten the effect of this activity, some teachers have used giant drawings of trees on the bulletin boards. You can then place the different names on branches, leaves, or apples.

Although this effort to help "ground" students in their family lineage is important, it must be acknowledged that for some students this is difficult because of their uniquely fluid family relationships. Teachers need to be sensitive to this and help those pupils identify uncles, grandparents, surrogate parents, and others who may play as vital a role in the students' life as their biological parents and relatives.

> *Our lives are shaped by those who love us—*
> *by those who refuse to love us.*
>
> John Powell, S.J.

Photo by Jack Wait

100

friends

One of the factors that erodes self-concept is the inability of some youngsters to make and keep friends. The following activities are designed to help the pupil expand his repertoire of skills in building and enhancing relationships with his peers.

1. Have the class discuss the methods they use to make friends. Take some time to brainstorm some new ways. Role-play the best ones.

2. Ask the students to draw a picture of a friend. Underneath the picture ask them to write a paragraph beginning with "A friend is. . ." Some students may protest that they have no friends. If this happens, ask them to draw a picture of friends they would like to have. You may wish to have the children share their paragraphs verbally or by posting their completed projects on the bulletin board.

3. Lead a class discussion around the following questions: Do you have a best friend? Do you like to do the same things? Did you ever want to do something that he didn't want to do? What happened? Were you still friends?

4. Ask the students to write a paragraph answering the following question: "What is there about you that makes your friend like you?"

5. Try out the following questions for discussion developed by William Glasser, author of *Schools Without Failure*. These questions are guaranteed to stimulate discussion:

How do you make friends? What is a friend? Do you have a friend? What makes a good friend? How do you find a friend? Is it better to have a lot of friends or just a few friends?

When you first came to school, how did you make a friend? Have you ever moved into a new neighborhood and had no friends at all? How did you find a friend there? What do you do when someone new moves into your neighborhood—do you wait for him to come over to your house or do you go over to his house and try to make friends with him? Do you ever make an effort to help him become friendly with other children?

I do then with my friends as I do with my books. I would have them where I can find them, but I seldom use them.

Ralph Waldo Emerson
"Friendship," *Essays: First Series* [1841]

101

class applause

The class applause exercise is a simple technique for cheering up a fellow class member. (It works for staff members too!) Often a student indicates frustration, discouragement, or some other feeling or behavior that lets you know he is "down." Sometimes you can sense that someone needs support; other times you might simply ask if there is anyone that would like a lift.

When a candidate for class applause has been identified, have everyone jump to their feet, clap their hands, and shout words of encouragement and affection for the "down" person. The applauders may hug or pat the recipient on the back to give further strength to the response.

Obviously this exercise can be futile or phoney if done insincerely or at the wrong time—but it can also lead to demonstrated caring for one's fellow class members. At other times it may be more efficacious to spend some time allowing the target person to simply talk about what is bothering him. Sometimes both processes are warranted and add to one another.

> . . .*every time you think you are not happy, say "I am happy." Say it strongly to yourself, even if your feelings are contradictory. Remember, it is your self-image and not you. Just as fast as a fish can move in the water, you can instantly change to a happy, balanced attitude.*
>
> Tarthang Tulku, Rinpoche
> *"The Self-Image"*

102

the car wash

A lovely little activity was introduced to one of our college classes recently by a student. He said it was called "Car Wash," and for very good reason, as you'll see.

The Car Wash consists simply of lining up your class or group in two parallel lines quite close together. Then one student is sent through the wash (between the lines) and everyone touches him or her and says words of praise and affection and encouragement. The pats on the back, hand-shaking, and verbal support produce a sparkling, shiny, happy "car" at the end of the wash!

We usually run one or two people through the car wash each day rather than everybody in one big clean-up. That insures that the responses of the washers are fresh, personalized, and enthusiastic.

> *What a strange machine man is! You fill him with bread, wine, fish, and radishes, and out of him come sighs, laughter, and dreams.*
>
> Nikos Kazantzakis
> *Zorba the Greek*

103

one-way feeling glasses

Our friend Gerry Weinstein developed this exercise and it's a good one. As the group leader, explain that you have some "magic glasses" for their eyes. You hold out your hands and "show" them, although they're invisible! (You might use inexpensive eye-glass frames.) Let each participant pretend to take a pair of glasses out of your hands and put them on. Then ask if they notice that these magic glasses enable them to see everything "through happy eyes." Everything looks nice, joyous—the world is a happy place. Have them interact on that basis.

When you think they're ready for a change, help them switch their glasses to "angry glasses." Now the world is an angry place. Everything that's done causes angry responses. The room is full of grouches. Again let them interact for a while.

At an appropriate time you may switch to other glasses such as:

Scared	Gloomy	Suspicious	Stubborn
Bragging	Things are OK	Modest	
Noboby loves me	Curious	Show-off	

After several role-playing situations, carry on a discussion of their feeling while wearing different types of glasses. Have there been days when they think you've had on a particular pair of one-way feeling glasses? Do they know people who seem to always wear one type of glasses? Probe for what the exercise may mean to them in their own daily behavior.

There is an excellent description of classroom work with one-way glasses in *Toward Humanistic Education: A Curriculum of Affect,* edited by Gerald Weinstein and Mario Fantini (New York: Praeger, 1970).

The aim was to have each student realize that restricting himself to a single view of people and situations limited his power, identity, and relations with others, and that if he could, through practice, learn to see some situations in new ways, he might find these to be more satisfying, potent, and useful than the old.

Gerald Weinstein and Mario Fantini
Toward Humanistic Education

104

"FRIENDLY" SENTENCE STUBS

The world would be a better place if everyone. . .

One thing I like about my friends is. . .

Cooperation is important because. . .

Other people are important because. . .

One thing I like to do in groups is. . .

I like my family because. . .

Helping others is. . .

My best friend can be counted on to. . .

If I could teach everyone in the world one thing, it would be. . .

I can help other people most by. . .

I like my best friend because. . .

I like my mother when. . .

When somebody is nice to me, I. . .

One way I am like everybody else is. . .

One way I am different from everyone else is. . .

A person I learn a lot from is. . .

One important thing I'm learning in school is. . .

One thing I could teach someone else is. . .

I like being with people when. . .

I like being with people who. . .

I like my parents when. . .

I come to you with a mind teeming with knowledge. . .and a heart swollen with love.
The former is of little use to you.
The latter will give you life!

Harold C. Wells

For Men Only:*
THE KEY TO HEALTH, WEALTH, AND LONGEVITY

Dr. Joyce Brothers

How would you like to be healthier, live longer, and earn more? Without having to go on a diet, do exercises, or work harder (or longer)? Sounds like a never-never idea, doesn't it? Well, there's a very simple prescription that will help you achieve these goals. It was worked out by a group of German psychologists, physicians, and insurance companies who cooperated on a research project designed to find out the secret of long life and success. They found, according to Dr. Arthur Szabo of West Germany, that the key to longer, happier, healthier, wealthier lives for men lies in one single act. All you have to do is:

KISS YOUR WIFE EACH MORNING
WHEN YOU LEAVE FOR WORK!

You don't have to *feel* like kissing her; just do it. That's the secret of success.

The meticulous German researchers discovered that men who kiss their wives every morning have fewer automobile accidents on their way to work then men who omit the morning kiss. The good-morning kissers miss less work because of sickness than the non-kissers. And they earn from 20 to 30 percent more money and live some five years longer than men who are stingy with their kisses.

Dr. Szabo explains, "A husband who kisses his wife every morning begins the day with a positive attitude."

Is there any hope for those gentlemen who neglect to deliver that morning kiss? They have a lot going against them, insists Dr. Szabo. These unaffectionate fellows start the day with negative feelings and doubts about their own worth. You see, a kiss is a kind of seal of approval.

If *you* have been rushing out of the house in the morning without kissing your wife, consider changing your ways. It might make a change in your wife, too. Why not try it?

---

*Editor's note: With all the changes in sex roles that are taking place, we imagine that this approach would prove equally effective for a woman kissing her husband before she leaves for work.

Photo by Janet Goto

105

spreading the effect

Because the students in your classes also interact with other teachers and staff in your school, it is advisable to seek ways to spread the influence of self-enhancement to your colleagues as well as your pupils. Here are a few ways you might go about this.

Give or lend a copy of this book to your principal and fellow teachers. Perhaps you can start a series of in-service sessions learning the techniques advocated in this book.

When you're eating lunch, ask the other teachers at your table what has been the point of their morning? By helping teachers focus on their own successes rather than their failures you will be helping spread positivity throughout the school. This is also a good way to begin a faculty meeting—to get the teachers focusing on the positive rather than the negative.

When you're filling out cumulative record forms at the end of the year, resist the temptation to release all of your pent-up resentments in the form of written diatribes on the children's forms. Instead, adopt the guideline that you will write about the child's growth; his strengths and his achievements. What you write will have a great effect on creating the next teacher's expectations of the student. When a "problem child" is being discussed, try to bring the discussion around to the child's strengths that can be built upon in the future, rather than all the events in the past which validate the teacher's feelings of hopelessness.

For teachers to help students develop positive self-concepts, they too need to feel positively about themselves. You can help develop this by looking for the strengths of your fellow teachers and telling them about them.

Resist the temptation to join in the negatively oriented "bitch sessions" that are so common to the teachers' lounge. Instead of griping about the past, try to focus the conversation on positive solutions to your problems.

Find a good idea that your principal, counselor, or fellow teacher has had and compliment him/her on it.

We all make mistakes. But to commit a wrong, to lower the dignity of a child and not be aware that the dignity has been impaired, is much more serious than the child's skipping words during reading.

Clark E. Moustakas

The Authentic Teacher

eight

in closing— new lyrics for old maladies

We've been at this book for a couple of years and we're still convinced that there is a prominent place for it in every teacher's, administrator's, and other group leader's bag. We're convinced because it is indeed a practical book and it deals with a fundamental need of our time—to enhance the identity and self-concept of people in groups.

A word about people in groups seems appropriate at this point because that's the way people seem to come these days—in groups. There are two general kinds of group leaders; those who have a continuing responsibility over an extended period, such as teachers, principals, church school teachers, scout leaders, and so on; and those whose responsibility is short-lived—from an hour or two to a couple of weeks. These latter are common today in the humanistic movement; they are like wandering minstrels, bringing new songs and dances, new styles of being, all with considerable fanfare to an eager audience. It is these minstrels who have created most of the exercises in this book, so our comments are not hostile. In fact, we do our share of this type of group leadership too. In any event, this book should be useful to those kinds of group leaders, except for the advanced sages of the esoteric, but it is really the former group—those whose work involves continuing relationships—that we had in mind and to whom we wish to direct these closing comments.

A leader coming in from Bora Bora with the latest discovery in "transintrospective actualizational meditation" can say to his quivering group, "All right, get on the floor on your backs with your eyes closed, fold your hands where they fall naturally below your navel, and get in touch with your body," and the group will dive to the floor with eager anticipation. But let the high school English teacher or elementary school principal try that and the repercussions are likely to be considerable—and immediate! So, a different style of working with continuing groups seems necessary. The style we advocate is open discussions—and plenty of them—daily, if possible. Time without agendas when leaders can stop being leaders and be people in groups with other people. Open discussion about whatever comes up. "How is it with you today, Mary?" "What can we do to improve our class?" "Why is the classroom becoming so noisy that last hour every day?" "I love this kind of quiet time we have together at the end of the day!" Can you see a group in which these questions or comments are raised by any group member? In this atmosphere the techniques described in this book can flow rather naturally to supplement and enhance feelings and relationships. In other words, *most* of the time is spent in open discussion.

Our position is not too unlike William Glasser's, as outlined in his *Schools Without Failure*. When he is referring to teachers working with students he talks about "classroom meetings." We call them "self-help groups." They are essentially the same except for our desire to have some skills, some "inputs," if you will, that push the process along a little faster. But we start with open meetings and end with open meetings; discussing and discussing; keeping the channels open for new insights to flow naturally at each individual's pace, depending on the readiness of each person for what is available in the environment.

The immediate aim is a clearer sense of identity and improved self-concept for individuals. This goal is optimized where a sense of community exists.

Jack Canfield
Harold Wells

annotated bibliography

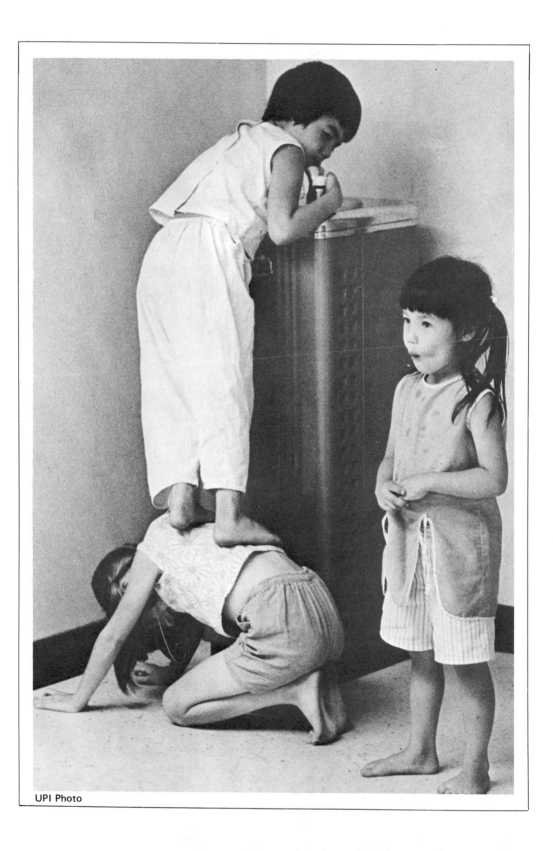

annotated bibliography of available resources

What follows is a very small bibliography when we consider all of the books, curricula, periodicals, and educational projects that deal directly with this very important issue of the student's self-concept. We have listed below those resources that have been the most useful to us. The guide contains annotated references to over 289 resources including books, curricula, classroom exercises, tapes, films, curriculum development projects, growth centers, and professional associations with special interest in the area of humanistic education.

1. Books that have had special meaning to us

Awareness, by John P. Stevens (Real People Press, Box F, Moab, Utah 84532, 1971, 275 pages; paperback, New York: Bantam Books, 1973, 309 pages). This is an excellent book combining theory and over 100 exercises drawn from Gestalt awareness training, almost all of which can be used in the classroom. The exercises include personal awareness, communication with others, fantasy journeys, exercises for couples and groups, exercises utilizing art, movement, and sound, and a special section entitled "To the Group Leader or Teacher." We highly recommend this book.

Anger and the Rocking Chair: Gestalt Awareness with Children, by Janet Lederman (New York: McGraw-Hill, 1969, 63 pages; paperback, New York: Viking Press, 1973, 63 pages). This book is a dramatic, visual account of the use of Gestalt methods with so-called "difficult" or "disturbed" children in an elementary school. Rather than suppressing students' rebellion and anger, Miss Lederman helps her pupils transform these powerful impulses into constructive attributes and behavior.

Born to Win: Transactional Analysis with Gestalt Experiments, by Muriel James and Dorothy Jongeward (Reading, Mass.: Addison-Wesley, 1971, 297 pages). This book is valuable in many ways. It contains a clear-cut statement of the theory of transactional analysis and its applications to everyday life, as well as Gestalt-oriented experiments to help people discover the many parts of their personality, to help them integrate them, and to help them develop an inner core of self-confidence. We have found this book very helpful in conceptualizing much of what we believe about self-concept work in the class.

Educational Implications of Self-Concept Theory, by Wallace D. LaBenne and Bert I. Greene (Pacific Palisades, Calif.: Goodyear Publishing Co., 1969, 134 pages). After a review of the classical self-concept literature, the authors spell out the implications of the literature for such educational issues as ability grouping, promotion practices, grading practices, classroom discipline, and evaluation.

Encounter with the Self, by Donald E. Hamachek (New York: Holt, Rinehart and Winston, 1971, 264 pages). Written for educators, this book is probably the most thorough statement of self-concept theory we know of. Filled with references to current research, case histories, anecdotal materials, and Peanuts cartoons, the book is both academically solid and eminently readable.

How Children Fail and *How Children Learn,* by John Holt (New York: Delta Books, 1966 and 1967). These two classic books by Holt have inspired a host of experiments in schooling. The first volume focuses on the strategies students use to cope with the pressures placed on them by the school system. Its discussion of the differences between real learning and apparent learning make it as relevant today as it was when it was written. The second volume concentrates on ways of nurturing children's emotional and mental growth.

In Search of Self, by Arthur T. Jersild (New York: Teachers College Press, 1952; also available in paperback). Subtitled "An Exploration of the Role of the School in Promoting Self-Understanding," this work is a pioneer effort in relating the goals of education to the quest for self-knowledge. His early insights are very helpful.

Perceiving, Behaving, and Becoming, ed. by Arthur W. Combs (Yearbook of the Association for Supervision and Curriculum Development, 1701 K Street, N.W., Washington, D.C. 20006, 1962). This book contains a series of articles by leading educational theorists in perception, self-concept, and self-actualization. Included are statements by Carl R. Rogers, Abraham H. Maslow, and Earl Kelley.

Psycho-Cybernetics, by Maxwell Maltz (Englewood Cliffs, N.J.: Prentice-Hall, 1960). Using real-life examples, the author shows how one can create a totally new image of himself as a successful and happy person. The use of creative imagery is a very important part of self-concept improvement. Maltz offers many suggestions along these lines.

Psychosynthesis: A Manual of Principles and Techniques, by Roberto Assagioli (New York: Hobbs, Dorman and Co., 1965; paperback, New York: Viking Press, 1970). Psychosynthesis is a way of pulling all the various trends in humanistic psychology and education together. It is an approach that fosters the balanced development of the body, feelings, mind, and spirit around a unifying center of being and awareness—the Transpersonal Self. Assagioli's work on "the ideal self" is very helpful in self-concept work.

Pygmalion in the Classroom: Teacher's Expectations and Pupil's Intellectual Development, by Robert Rosenthal and L. Jacobsen (New York: Holt, Rinehart and Winston, 1968). Rosenthal and Jacobsen report their research, indicating that whatever a teacher expects from a student she will probably get. The need for the teacher to "believe in" the child's ability to succeed is amply supported by their work.

Schools Without Failure, by William Glasser (New York: Harper & Row, 1969, 235 pages). Glasser offers a new approach to reduce school failures—an approach based on personal involvement, relevance, and thinking. Through the use of the "classroom meeting" (mentioned earlier) he demonstrates how to reach negatively oriented, failure-conscious students and how to help them to aim for positive goal-setting, personal achievement, and individual responsibility.

Self-Concept and School Achievement, by William W. Purkey (Englewood Cliffs, N.J.: Prentice-Hall, 1970, 86 pages). Purkey explores the growing emphasis on the student's subjective and personal evaluation of himself as a dominant influence on his success or failure in school. He explains how the self-concept develops in social interaction and what happens to it in school. He also suggests ways for the teacher to reinforce positive and realistic self-concepts in students. Because of its ease in reading, we very often suggest it as helpful to give to parents from whom you are trying to enlist support for an affective education program.

Teacher and Child, by Haim G. Ginott (New York: Macmillan, 1972, 323 pages). Ginott goes beyond mere theory and offers teachers a model for a language of acceptance and compassion: words that convey feelings, responses that change moods, statements that invite good will, answers that bring insight, replies that radiate respect, and, in general, a language that lingers lovingly. Ginott's suggestions are designed to increase a child's sense of self-worth and to enhance the quality of life in the classroom. The chapter in which he distinguishes between evaluative and appreciative praise is particularly valuable reading.

The Antecedents of Self-Esteem, by Stanley Coopersmith (San Francisco: W. H. Freeman & Co., 1967). This is a doctoral dissertation on the self-esteem of a group of junior high boys. It is academic reading, but the conclusions listed at the end of each chapter are well worth reading.

The Self-Concept: A Critical Survey of Pertinent Research Literature, by Ruth Wylie (Lincoln, Nebraska: University of Nebraska Press, 1961). This book contains a critical review of all of the self-concept research done through 1961. Although a bit dated, it offers valuable information for those trying to communicate self-concept work in the classroom to school boards, parents, etc.

Values and Teaching: Working with Values in the Classroom, by Louis E. Raths, Merrill Harmin, and Sidney B. Simon (Columbus, Ohio: Charles E. Merrill, 1966, 275 pages). This book, one of our earlier bibles, outlines a theory of values and a classroom methodology for the clarification of values. It contains many practical classroom activities that teachers can employ to help students clarify their values.

Values Clarification: A Handbook of Practical Strategies for Teachers and Students, by Sidney B. Simon, Leland W. Howe, and Howard Kirschenbaum (New York: Hart Publishing Co., 1972, 397 pages). This extremely practical book contains seventy-nine classroom exercises designed to help students clarify their values. Each exercise is clearly written and contains many examples of ways in which it can be used. This book promises to become a classic in humanistic education. It belongs in your basic library!

Your Child's Self-Esteem, by Dorothy Corkille Briggs (Garden City, N.Y.: Doubleday, 1970, 341 pages). We are very enthusiastic about this gem of a book! It's probably the best book on self-concept for parents that we know of. We highly recommend it to both parents and teachers.

2. Books we recommend for parents

Between Parent and Child and *Between Parent and Teenager,* by Haim G. Ginott (New York: Macmillan, 1969).

Dibs: In Search of Self, by Virginia M. Axline (New York: Ballantine Books, 1967).

Helping Your Child Develop His Potentialities, by Ruth Strang (New York: E.P. Dutton, 1965; paperback, New York: Award Books, 1970).

I'm OK; You're OK, by Tom Harris (New York: Harper & Row, 1070). A primer on transactional analysis.

Living with Children: New Methods for Parents and Teachers, by G. Patterson and Elizabeth Gallion (Research Press, 2612 North Mattis Ave., Champaign, Ill. 61820). A positive approach using behavior modification methods.

Parent Effectiveness Training, by Tom Gordon (New York: Peter H. Wyden, Publisher, 1970); and *Teacher Effectiveness Training* (New York: Peter H. Wyden, Publisher, 1974).

Peoplemaking (because you want to be a better parent), by Virginia Satir (Palo Alto, Calif.: Science and Behavior Books, 1972).

3. Self-concept curriculum materials

About Me: A Curriculum for a Developing Self, by Harold Wells, and John T. Canfield (Encyclopedia Britannica Education Corporation, 425 North Michigan Avenue, Chicago, Illinois 60611). This inexpensive curriculum is designed to help children in grades 4 to 6 develop positive self-concepts. Lessons include I Know Who I Am, I Know My Strengths, I Can Set and Achieve Goals, I Try to Be Myself, and I Am in Charge of Becoming Myself. Since we wrote it, we think it's pretty good!

Achievement Competence Training, by Russell A. Hill and the Staff of the Humanizing Learning Program of Research for Better Schools, Inc. (Research for Better Schools, Suite 1700, 1700 Market Street, Philadelphia, Pa. 19103). ACT is a comprehensive learning package designed to teach students a variety of strategies for setting and reaching their goals. Hill and his colleagues have developed a really solid program to enhance students' self-motivation, self-confidence, and self-actualization. The program is a bit expensive but well worth looking into.

Achievement Motivation Materials, by Alfred Alschuler, Diane Tabor, and James McIntyre (Education Ventures, Inc., 209 Court Street, Middletown, Conn. 06457). These materials were adapted for ninth-grade use from those developed by the Achievement Motivation Development Project at Harvard University. Brief teachers' guides accompany the materials and suggest variations for their use.

Developing Understanding of Self and Others (DUSO), by Don Dinkmeyer (American Guidance Service, Inc., Dept. EL-4, Publishers' Building, Circle Pines, Minn. 55014). This is a program designed to help elementary children understand themselves and others around them. The DUSO kits provide a wide variety of experiences designed to reach children with unique learning styles through varied media and modes.

Dimensions of Personality Series, by Walter J. Limbacher (George A. Pflaum, Pub., 38 West Fifth Street, Dayton, Ohio 45402). This series is based on the belief that the classroom teacher can be an enormously successful partner in helping youngsters live happy and useful lives. The program is experiential and discussion-centered, built around a book of very good readings for each grade level. The books include *Here I Am* (grade 4), *I'm Not Alone* (grade 5), and *Becoming Myself* (grade 6). They've recently published books for the lower grades and grade seven as well.

Focus on Self Development, by Judith L. Anderson, Carole J. Lang, and Virginia R. Scott (Science Research Associates, 259 East Erie Street, Chicago, Illinois 60611). This is a developmental affective educational program for grades one through three. The overall objectives are to lead the child toward an understanding of self, an understanding of others, and an understanding of the environment and its effects on him. It includes filmstrips, records, photoboards, pupil activity books, and a teacher's guide.

The Human Development Program, by Uvaldo Palomares, Geraldine Ball, and Harold Bessell (Human Development Training Institute, 7574 University Avenue, La Mesa, Calif. 92041). This program is designed to facilitate learning in the affective domain, thereby improving motivation and achievement in all areas of education. The strategy is to employ cumulative, sequential activities on a daily basis as outlined in the teacher lesson guides.

I Have Feelings, by Terry Berger (Behavioral Publications, 2852 Broadway, New York, N.Y. 10025). Covering seventeen different feelings, both good and bad, and the situations that precipitated each one, the book is geared for children ages 4 to 9.

Kids Magazine (747) Third Avenue, New York, N.Y. 10017). *Kids* is a great new magazine written *by* kids *for* kids.

Motivation Advance Program, by Audrey J. Peterson (Achievement Motivation System, 111 E. Wacker Drive, Chicago, Ill. 60601). This program provides experiences and information to assist young people in expanding their attitudes toward self-acceptance as worthwhile, unique individuals. Designed for junior high and high school, the program includes establishing group rapport, analyzing achievement patterns, identifying untapped personal resources, clarifying values, setting goals, and managing conflict.

Self-Enhancing Education: A Program to Motivate Learners, by Norma Randolph and William Howe (Sanford Press, Palo Alto, Cal.). This book describes a program which teachers may use to help their students grow in self-esteem through practical and effective processes.

4. Periodicals you might wish to subscribe to

Confluent Education Newsletter, c/o Confluent Education Program, Box 219, Minnedosa, Manitoba, Canada, is published periodically by the Confluent Education Project. Confluent Education refers to the "flowing together of the affective and the cognitive domains." We have found this little newsletter full of good ideas.

Learning Magazine, 530 University Avenue, Palo Alto, Calif. 94301, is consistently the best major magazine in education that we read each month. It is full of useful articles on new approaches to teaching, new materials available, and new ways of conceptualizing the teaching-learning process. In a recent publicity piece the magazine was described as one that "simply gives you a good *feeling*—about yourself, your kids and the job you're trying so hard to do for them."

Media and Methods, 134 N. 13th Street, Philadelphia, Pa. 19107, always contains its fair share of articles about humanizing the learning process. *M&M* is of special interest to teachers of English and teachers using film-making and movies in their teaching.

People Watching: Curriculum and Techniques for Teaching the Behavioral Sciences in the Classroom, Behavioral Publications, 2852 Broadway, New York, N.Y. 10025, is a recent quarterly publication featuring articles, techniques, reviews, and programs that deal with aspects of the behavioral sciences and their application in the classroom.

5. Organizations you should know about

We suggest that you buy a stack of postcards, address them to the following organizations, and ask them to place you on their mailing lists. The materials you receive will keep you very up to date as to what is going on and how these organizations might best serve your efforts to improve the self-concepts of the students you work with.

Sagamore Institute, 110 Spring Street, Saratoga Springs, N.Y. 12866. In addition to conducting seminars in humanistic education and value clarification, the Center has available reprints of many books and articles in the area of value clarification by Sidney B. Simon and others.

Affective Education Development Project, Room 323, Philadelphia Board of Education, Twenty-first and Parkway, Philadelphia, Pa. 19103 (Norman Newberg, Director). This project has been developing curricula and providing in-service teacher training in affective education in the Philadelphia area. It is the most extensive urban affective education project in the country.

Association for Humanistic Psychology, 325 Ninth Street, San Francisco, Calif. 94103, is a tremendously useful organization to belong to. In addition to publishing a monthly newsletter and the *Journal of Humanistic Psychology,* AHP holds annual national and regional conferences that are unparalleled in bringing together top-notch people who are working in the areas of humanistic education and psychology. The Association also publishes a series of "Paper Dragons" (reprinted articles and other materials related to humanistic education).

The Barksdale Foundation, Idyllwild, Calif. 92348, "is a non-profit, self-funding organization devoted to helping people live happier, more effective lives. This is accomplished through achieving better understanding of how and why we get involved in emotional turmoil, and why we often have a destructive sense of inadequacy and self-rejection. The primary emphasis is on assisting people to build sound self-esteem and confidence in themselves and their own authority." Anyone interested in their material may receive it free of charge as it becomes available, if they will send a written request to Foundation headquarters.

The Center for Humanistic Education, University of Massachusetts, Amherst, Mass. 01002 (Gerald Weinstein, Director). The Center offers graduate and undergraduate courses in Education of the Self, Values Clarification, Humanistic Curriculum Development, Theory of Psychological Education, Strength Training, and Combatting White Racism. The Center is also involved in an extensive curriculum development project, funded by the Ford Foundation, to produce and implement psychological curricula to deal with the student's concerns of identity, interpersonal relationships (connectedness), and personal power.

Center for Humanistic Education, Norman Hall, University of Florida, Gainesville, Fl. 32061 (William W. Purkey, Director), was recently created to "assist school districts (and other institutions) in finding practical solutions to dehumanizing problems, to disseminate information on humanistic education, to conduct research in developing and substantiating the theory and practice of humanizing approaches to education." Purkey, as you may have noted, is the author of *Self-Concept and School Achievement.*

Center for Theatre Techniques in Education, American Shakespeare Festival Theatre, Stratford, Conn. 06497 (Mary Hunter Wolf, Director), has been developing innovative techniques for self-concept development using theatre techniques since 1969. The foundation of the techniques employed is the use of improvisations and theatre games to build better communication, quicker response, and creative interaction in the classroom. Staff training workshops are conducted, and a book of theatre games is currently being assembled.

Development and Research in Confluent Education (DRICE), Department of Education, University of California, Santa Barbara, Calif. 93106 (George I. Brown, Director), is developing curricula and training teachers in the area of confluent education. Its aim is to integrate the knowledge and activities of the human potential movement with the traditional classroom curriculum, thus creating a more holistic learning situation for students. The basic work of DRICE is reported in George Brown's books *Human Teaching for Human Learning* (New York: The Viking Press, 1971); and *The Live Classroom: Innovation through Confluent Education and Gestalt* (New York: The Viking Press, 1975).

Educator Training Center, 2140 West Olympic Boulevard, Los Angeles, Calif. 90006, was created by William Glasser to research ideas and develop methods for combating school failure. Building primarily on a process called the "classroom meeting," ETC has developed a practical in-service program which any elementary school can use to help eliminate failure by building the self-worth of the students through effective communication and motivation.

Effectiveness Training Association, 110 East Euclid, Pasadena, Calif. 91101 (Dr. Thomas Gordon, Director), is an organization whose object is to "provide educational experience for people who want to learn the specific skills required to develop and foster effective human relationships in which people can fulfill their own potential, help others to fulfill theirs and resolve their conflicts in a spirit of mutal respect, in friendship, and in peace." Courses are offered in parent-effectiveness training, teacher-effectiveness training, and leader-effectiveness training.

Institute for Humanistic Education, 535, St. Paul Place, Baltimore, Md. 21202 (Barbara Raines, Director), is involved in training teachers to implement humanistic education, It also helps teachers to form support groups for mutually exploring more humanistic ways of teaching.

Self-Esteem Seminars, 17156 Palisades Circle, Pacific Palisades, CA 90272 (Jack Canfield, President), conducts personal and professional development workshops, teacher training and consulting services in the area of self-esteem.

TORI Associates, Inc., P.O. Box 694, La Jolla, Calif. 92038, is an international non-profit organization, devoted to continuing discovery of ways to enrich community living. Jack Gibb and his associates have a keen interest in the application of TORI principles to education.

Values Associates, P.O. Box 43, Amherst, Mass. 01002, is a team of educational consultants (directed by Sid Simon, co-author of *Values and Teaching* and *Values Clarification)* who have spent many years working with teachers, students, parents, and churches in the area of values clarification. Send for their brochure describing weekend workshops as well as their consulting services.

Youth Research Foundation, 122 West Franklin Avenue, Minneapolis, Minn. 55404, has long been involved in designing and conducting programs for youth, teachers, and parents in the areas of value clarification, positive self-actualization, and human relations training. It also sponsors programs in parent-effectiveness training.

6. Growth centers we have known

Almost any experience of teachers, counselors, and administrators at a growth center is beneficial to the eventual improvement of self-concepts in the classroom. Personal growth experiences help you become more aware of your own emotional life and the effect of your behavior on others (i.e., your students). Personal growth groups also promote your own growth and self-actualization, thus allowing you to be more in touch with your deeper feelings about yourself and your students.

Above and beyond the many general workshops in encounter, Gestalt, sensory awareness, massage, theatre games, psychosynthesis, bio-energetics, and transactional analysis, many growth centers are now conducting programs specifically for educators. You can get a free list of the over 145 growth centers across the country by writing AHP, 325 Ninth Street, San Francisco, Calif. 94103, and ask for its growth center list.

We have listed below several of the growth centers that have addressed themselves more directly to affective/humanistic education. We suggest that you write for their current brochures.

Cambridge House, 1900 N. Cambridge Avenue, Milwaukee, Wis. 53202, always includes several workshops focusing on the personal and professional growth of teachers in its program.

Center for the Studies of the Person, 1125 Torrey Pines Road, La Jolla, Calif. 92037, was founded by Carl Rogers (author of *Freedom to Learn*). The Center is involved in several major projects to implement humanistic education in the schools.

Esalen Institute, Big Sur, Calif. 93920, is the oldest growth center in the country. Its programs are the most extensive offered of any growth center we know of; the Institute always has a host of programs in the area of confluent and humanistic education.

National Center for the Exploration of Human Potential, 976 Chalcedony Street, San Diego, Calif. 92109, is very involved in both training and research in the area of humanistic education.

OASIS, 6 West Ontario Street, Chicago, Ill. 60610, is the major growth center in the Midwest. It sponsors a wide range of growth programs, including seminars in affective education.

QUEST, 4933 Auburn Avenue, Bethesda, Md. 20014, has been sponsoring workshops in humanistic education with Hal Lyon, author of *Learning to Feel—Feeling to Learn.*

ACKNOWLEDGMENTS

We would like to acknowledge publishers and individuals for permission to reprint the following:

QUOTATIONS

Pages xvii and 95
The Psychology of Self-Esteem by Nathaniel Branden (Plainview, N.Y.: Nash Publishing Corporation). Copyright © 1969 by Nathaniel Branden. Reprinted by permission of Gerard McCauley Agency, Inc.

Page xvii
"The Burnt Flower Bed" by Ugo Betti. Copyright © by Andreina Betti. Reprinted by permission of Grove Press, Inc. and Curtis Brown Ltd.

Page xvii
Man, the Manipulator by Everett Shostrom (Nashville, Tenn.: Abingdon Press, 1967). Reprinted by permission of the author and Abingdon Press.

Page 5
"Self-Actualizing People: A Study of Psychological Health" by Abraham H. Maslow, in *The Self: Explorations in Personal Growth,* Clark E. Moustakas, editor (New York: Harper & Row, Publishers, Inc., 1956). Reprinted by permission of Grune & Stratton, Inc.

Pages 6 and 141
About Me: A Curriculum for a Developing Self by Harold Wells and Jack Canfield. Excerpt reprinted by permission of Encyclopedia Britannica Educational Corporation, 425 North Michigan Avenue, Chicago, Illinois 60611.

Pages 6, 104, and 113
Encounter with the Self by Donald E. Hamachek (New York: Holt, Rinehart and Winston, Inc., 1971). Reprinted by permission of the author and Holt, Rinehart and Winston, Inc.

Page 11
Neurotic Distortion of the Creative Process by Lawrence S. Kubie (New York: Farrar, Straus & Giroux, Inc., Noonday Press, 1967), p. 133. Copyright © 1958/1961 by the University of Kansas Press. Reprinted by permission of Farrar, Straus & Giroux, Inc.

Page 12
"Children Learn What They Live" by Dorothy Law Nolte. Copyright Dorothy Law Nolte. Reprinted by permission of the author.

Pages 17 and 203
Love and Will by Rollo May. Copyright © 1969 by W. W. Norton & Company, Inc. Reprinted by permission of the author, W. W. Norton & Company, Inc., and Souvenir Press Ltd.

Pages 18 and 19
"Love and the Cabbie" by Art Buchwald. Copyright The Washington Post Co. Reprinted by permission of the author and Los Angeles Times Syndicate.

Page 23
Poem by Charles Finnegan, fifth-grade student of Katherine Lee Bates School, Wellesley, Mass., 1970. Reprinted by permission of Charles Finnegan and his parents.

Page 27
Here Comes Everybody by William C. Schutz, p. xviii. Copyright © 1971 by William C. Schutz. Reprinted by permission of Harper & Row, Publishers, Inc. and Sterling Lord Agency, Inc.

Pages 29, 55, and 94
Handbook for the Human Relations Approach to Teaching, published by the Human Relations Education Center of the Buffalo Public Schools, James J. Foley, Director. Published by permission of James J. Foley.

Page 29
The Razor's Edge by W. Somerset Maugham. Copyright 1943, 1944 by McCall Corporation. Copyright 1944 by W. Somerset Maugham. Reprinted by permission of Doubleday & Company, Inc., the Estate of W. Somerset Maugham, and William Heinemann, Ltd.

Page 31
The Prophet by Kahlil Gibran (New York: Alfred A. Knopf, Inc., 1923). Copyright 1923 by Kahlil Gibran; renewal copyright 1951 by Administrators C.T.A. of Kahlil Gibran's Estate and Mary G. Gibran. Reprinted by permission of Alfred A. Knopf, Inc.

Page 32
Educator's Handbook of Stories, Quotes, and Humor by Dale Baughman (Englewood Cliffs, N.J.: Prentice-Hall, Inc.). © 1963 by Prentice-Hall, Inc. Reprinted by permission of Prentice-Hall, Inc.

Page 33
Joy by William C. Schutz. Copyright © by William C. Schutz. Reprinted by permission of the author, Grove Press, Inc., and Souvenir Press Ltd.

Page 35
Excerpt from a public speech by Rev. Jesse Jackson. Used by permission of the author.

Page 39
Excerpt by Abraham H. Maslow in the *Yearbook* of the Association for Supervision and Curriculum Development *Perceiving, Behaving, and Becoming,* Arthur W. Combs, editor. Reprinted by permission of the Association for Supervision and Curriculum Development.

Pages 40, 53, 138, 177, and 187
The Annotated Alice: Alice's Adventures in Wonderland and through the Looking Glass by Lewis Carroll, illustrated by John Tenniel, with an introduction and notes by Martin Gardner. © 1960 by Martin Gardner. Used by permission of Clarkson N. Potter, Inc.

Page 41
Human Values in the Classroom: Teaching for Personal and Social Growth by Robert C. Hawley (Amherst, Mass.: Education Research Associates, 1973), p. 89. Reprinted by permission of the author and the publisher.

Pages 42 and 52
"Self-Awareness and the Social Studies" by Marlowe Berg and Patricia Wolleat. Unpublished manuscript, reprinted by permission of the author.

Page 42
Society and the Adolescent Self-Image by Morris Rosenberg (Princeton University Press, 1965; Princeton Paperback, 1968): selections on pp. 281-82. Reprinted by permission of Princeton University Press.

Page 43
Notes to Myself by Hugh Prather (Moab, Utah: Real People Press). Reprinted by permission of Real People Press.

Page 45
Quote from *Popeye the Sailor Man.* © King Features Syndicate, Inc. Used by permission of King Features Syndicate, Inc.

Page 84
"Positive Reinforcement: An Instructional Solution" by Noel McInnis, in a *Newsletter* of the Association for Humanistic Psychology. Reprinted by permission of the author and the Association for Humanistic Psychology.

Page 87
Crisis in the Classroom: The Remaking in American Education by Charles E. Silberman (New York: Random House, Inc., 1970). Copyright © 1970 by Charles E. Silberman. Reprinted by permission of Random House, Inc. and William Morris Agency, Inc.

Page 89
"Human Potential" by Herbert A. Otto and John Mann in *Human Potentialities*, Herbert A. Otto, editor (St. Louis: Warren H. Green, Inc., 1968), p. 143. Reprinted by permission of the author and Warren H. Green, Inc.

Page 90
"The Animal School" by George H. Reavis. Reprinted by permission of Phi Delta Kappa.

Page 93
Schools without Failure by William Glasser, p. 13. Copyright © 1969 by William Glasser, Inc. Reprinted by permission of the author and Harper & Row, Publishers, Inc.

Page 98
The Magic Monastery by Idries Shah (New York: E. P. Dutton & Co., Inc., 1972), p. 188. Copyright © 1972 by Idries Shah. Reprinted by permission of Collins-Knowlton-Wing, Inc. and Jonathan Cape, Ltd.

Page 99
The Knowledge of Man by Martin Buber, p. 71. Copyright © 1965 by Martin Buber and Maurice S. Friedman. Reprinted by permission of Harper & Row, Publishers, Inc. and George Allen & Unwin Ltd.

Page 100
Exercise suggested in the September, 1973 issue of *Swap Shop* by Astrid Collins, Markham Jr. High School, San Jose, California. © 1973 by Education Today Company, Inc., 530 University Avenue, Palo Alto, California 94301. Reprinted by special permission of *Learning*, The Magazine for Creative Teaching, September, 1973.

Page 100
Excerpt from *Pygmalion* by George Bernard Shaw. Reprinted by permission of The Society of Authors on behalf of the Bernard Shaw Estate.

Page 101
"What is Real?" from *The Velveteen Rabbit* by Margery Williams. Reprinted by permission of Doubleday & Company, Inc. and William Heinemann, Ltd.

Page 105
"Cognizantability" in *Gems of Wisdom* by Master Subramuniya (Virginia City, Nev.: Comstock House), p. 227. Reprinted by permission of the author and Comstock House.

Page 107
Excerpt from *Le Misanthrope* by Molière.

Pages 111 and 139
In Search of Self by Arthur T. Jersild (New York: Teachers College Press, 1952). Reprinted by permission of Teachers College Press.

Page 115
The Transparent Self by Sidney M. Jourard. © 1971. Reprinted by permission of the author and D. Van Nostrand Company.

Page 120
Excerpt by George Steiner in *Encounter* Magazine, London. Reprinted by permission of the author and the publisher.

Page 121
"Red Is. . . " by Anna Schneider. Reprinted by permission from *Kids,* The Magazine by Kids for Kids, Issue No. 2. Copyright 1971 by Childpub Management Corporation.

Page 123
Psychotherapy East and West by Alan Watts (New York: Pantheon Books, 1961), p. 15. Copyright © by Pantheon Books, a Division of Random House, Inc. Reprinted by permission of Pantheon Books.

Page 125
North Carolina Advanced Schools *Newsletter* by Dr. A. Craig Phillips, North Carolina State Superintendent of Public Instruction. Reprinted by permission of the author.

Page 129
"Schools Hire Out the Job of Teaching" by Bernard Asbell, *Think* Magazine, Sept./Oct., 1970. Reprinted by permission from *Think* Magazine, published by IBM, copyright 1970 by International Business Machines Corporation.

Page 130
"I Used to . . . But Now" by Oscar Marcilla. Reprinted by permission from *Kids,* The Magazine by Kids for Kids, Issue No. 14. Copyright 1972 by Childpub Management Corporation.

Page 137
E. E. Cummings: A Miscellany, George Firmage, editor. Reprinted by permission of Harcourt Brace Jovanovich, Inc.

Page 138
Improvisation for the Theatre by Viola Spolin (Evanston, Ill.: Northwestern University Press, 1963), p. 3. Reprinted by permission of Northwestern University Press.

Page 145
Awareness by John O. Stevens (Moab, Utah: Real People Press). Reprinted by permission of the author and the publisher.

Pages 147 and 163
The Betrayal of the Body by Alexander Lowen (New York: Macmillan Publishing Company, Inc., 1967). Copyright © 1967 by Alexander Lowen, M.D. Reprinted by permission of the author and Macmillan Publishing Company, Inc.

Page 153
You Are not the Target by Laura Huxley (New York: Farrar, Straus & Giroux, Inc., 1963). Copyright 1963 by Laura Huxley. Reprinted by permission of the author and the publisher.

Page 157
Unpublished mimeographed paper by Jack R. Gibb. Reprinted by permission of the author.

Page 159
Born to Win: Transactional Analysis with Gestalt Experiments by Muriel James and Dorothy

Jongeward (Reading, Mass.: Addison-Wesley Publishing Company, Inc., 1971). Reprinted by permission of the publisher.

Page 161
Psycho-Cybernetics by Maxwell Maltz (Englewood Cliffs, N.J.: Prentice-Hall, Inc.). © 1960 by Prentice-Hall, Inc. Reprinted by permission of Prentice-Hall, Inc.

Pages 164 and 165
Sense Relaxation by Bernard Gunther (New York: Macmillan Publishing Company, Inc.). Copyright © 1968 by Bernard Gunther. Reprinted by permission of Macmillan Publishing Company, Inc. and International Creative Management.

Page 167
Depression and the Body by Alexander Lowen (New York: Coward, McCann & Geoghegan, Inc., 1972). Copyright © by Alexander Lowen, M.D. Reprinted by permission of the author, Coward, McCann & Geoghegan, Inc., and Raines & Raines.

Page 179
"When I Grow up" by Jocelyn Shorin. Reprinted by permission from *Kids*, The Magazine by Kids for Kids, Issue No. 14. Copyright 1972 by Childpub Management Corporation.

Page 181
Unpublished mimeographed paper by Elaine Kepner and Lois Brien. Reprinted by permission of the author.

Page 184
Martin Buber: The Life and Dialogue by Maurice S. Friedman. Copyright © 1955, 1960 by Maurice S. Friedman. Reprinted by permission of The University of Chicago Press and Routledge & Kegan Paul Ltd.

Pages 188 and 189
Choose Success: How to Set and Achieve All Your Goals by Billy B. Sharp and Claire Cox (New York: Hawthorn Books, Inc.). Reprinted by permission of the author and Hawthorn Books, Inc.

Page 191
The Art of Loving by Erich Fromm, pp. 58-59, Vol. 9 of World Perspectives Series, planned and edited by Ruth Nanda Anshen. Copyright © 1956 by Erich Fromm. Reprinted by permission of Harper & Row, Publishers, Inc. and George Allen & Unwin Ltd.

Page 194
"Is Is What Was Was?" by Tom Hicks. Reprinted from *ETC.: A Review of General Semantics*, Vol. 28, No. 3 by permission of the International Society for General Semantics.

Pages 197 and 200
The Center of the Cyclone: An Autobiography of Inner Space by John C. Lilly M.D. (New York: Julian Press, 1972; Bantam Paperback, 1974). Reprinted by permission of The Julian Press, Inc.

Page 201
"I Taught Them All" by Naomi White. Reprinted from *Progressive Education*, November, 1943.

Page 205
Unpublished mimeographed paper by Lorraine M. Gibb. Reprinted by permission of the author.

Page 218
Between Parent and Child by Haim G. Ginott (New York: Macmillan Publishing Company, Inc., 1965), p. 125. Reprinted by permission of Dr. Alice Ginott. Other books of Dr. Haim G. Ginott are *Between Parent and Teenager* (Macmillan, 1969) and *Teacher and Child* (Macmillan, 1972).

Page 221
"Friendship" in *Essays: First Series* (1841) by Ralph Waldo Emerson.

Page 222
"The Self-Image" by Tarthang Tulku, Rinpoche. Copyright 1974, Transpersonal Institute, 2637 Marshall Drive, Palo Alto, California 94303. Reprinted by permission from Volume 6, Number 2 of the *Journal of Transpersonal Psychology.*

Page 223
Zorba the Greek by Nikos Kazantzakis. Copyright © 1952 by Simon & Schuster, Inc. Reprinted by permission of Simon & Schuster, Inc. and Dr. Max Tau for Mrs. Kazantzakis.

Page 225
Toward Humanistic Education: A Curriculum of Affect by Gerald Weinstein and Mario Fantini (New York: Praeger Publishers, Inc., 1970). © 1970 by the Ford Foundation. Reprinted by permission of the author and Praeger Publishers, Inc.

Page 227
The Brothers System for Liberated Love and Marriage by Joyce Brothers. Copyright by Dr. Joyce Brothers. Published by Peter H. Wyden, Publishers and reprinted by their permission.

Page 230
The Authentic Teacher: Sensitivity and Awareness in the Classroom by Clark E. Moustakas (Cambridge, Mass.: Howard A. Doyle, 1966). Copyright 1966 Clark E. Moustakas. Reprinted by permission of the author and Howard A. Doyle.

ILLUSTRATIONS

Page xviii
"Peanuts" cartoon by Charles M. Schulz. © 1971 United Feature Syndicate, Inc.

Pages 24, 108, 196, 208, and 216
Line drawing, reprinted from *I Am Twelve Years Old and I'm Glad* by Lawrence J. Branagan and Christopher Moroney, published by the Natick, Mass. Public School System. Copyright Lawrence J. Branagan and Christopher Moroney. Used by permission of the authors.

Page 28
Cartoon by Vahan Shirvanian. Copyright 1971 Saturday Review, Inc. Reprinted by permission of Vahan Shirvanian and Saturday Review, Inc.

Page 30
Cartoon by Sidney Harris. Copyright 1970. Reprinted by permission of Sidney Harris and Saturday Review, Inc.

Page 34
Cartoon by Chon Day. Copyright 1970. Reprinted by permission of Chon Day and Saturday Review, Inc.

Page 40
Line drawing "Alice and the Mad Hatter." Taken from *The Annotated Alice: Alice's Adventures in Wonderland and through the Looking Glass* by Lewis Carroll, illustrated by John Tenniel, with an introduction and notes by Martin Gardner. © 1960 by Martin Gardner. Used by permission of Clarkson N. Potter, Inc.

Page 44
Cartoon by Paul Peter Porges. Copyright February 6, 1971. Reprinted by permission of Paul Peter Porges and Saturday Review, Inc.

Page 46

Line drawing. This drawing is used by permission of Research Press, 2612 North Mattis Ave., Champaign, Illinois 61820. Research Press publishes many books in the area of humanistic education. We suggest you write for the catalog.

Page 66

"Peanuts" cartoon by Charles M. Schulz, © 1959 United Feature Syndicate, Inc.

Page 74

"Wee Pals" cartoon. © King Features Syndicate, Inc., 1975.

Page 88

"Peanuts" cartoon by Charles M. Schulz. © 1959 United Feature Syndicate, Inc.

Page 110

"Peanuts" cartoon by Charles M. Schulz, © 1960 United Feature Syndicate, Inc.

Page 112

Cartoon by Henry R. Martin. © 1971. Reprinted by permission of Henry R. Martin and Saturday Review, Inc.

Page 124

Cartoon by Bruce Cochran. Reproduced by special permission of *Playboy* Magazine; copyright © 1971 by Playboy.

Page 128

Short and Weaver cartoon. By permission of Short and Weaver Cartoons, Rowlesburg, West Virginia.

Page 132

Line drawings by Scott Armstrong and Brad Hish. Reprinted by permission from *Kids*, The Magazine by Kids for Kids, Issue No. 5. Copyright 1971 by Childpub Management Corporation.

Page 170

Cartoon by Herbert Goldberg. © 1970. Reprinted by permission of Herbert Goldberg and Saturday Review, Inc.

Page 176

Line drawings "Wishes from the Second Grade" by Bob, Wendy, Karen, Patricia, Jonathan, and Robert. Reprinted by permission from *Kids*, The Magazine by Kids for Kids, Issue No. 4. Copyright 1971 by Childpub Management Corporation.

Page 190

Line drawing and poem by Elaine Beaulieu. Reprinted by permission from *Kids*, The Magazine by Kids for Kids, Issue No. 3. Copyright 1971 by Childpub Management Corporation.

Page 194

Line drawing reproduced by permission of Noll C. Derriksan, Toussowasket '69, Westbank, British Columbia.

PHOTOGRAPHS

Pages 16, 20, 54, 60, 80, 92, 106, 116, 122, 158, 160, 174, 206, and 224
Photo by Ginny Duff.

Pages 36, 56, 136, 186, and 234
UPI.